INDOOR ROWING

PERFECTION IN EXERCISE

JAY NITHUS

Manufactured in the United States of America

CONTENTS

Introduction

Rowing is not exactly new, -records of its existence date back well over 1,000 years before the birth of Christ. At least that is what the records tell us; truthfully speaking, rowing most certainly has far longer history, one stretching back to the farthest reaches of antiquity; an antiquity never recorded one never heard of. Food supply, travel, warfare, -not to mention entertainment, were mainstays of rowing's very early and mostly pragmatic nature. The practicality of rowing's past speaks little of its current day usage as a sport. Competition or sport, by whatever definition, have always existed and this remains true for even for the most ancient practitioners; for even they were judged in terms of prowess. While tracing rowing's earliest steps provides for historical interest, elongated attempts uncovering rowing's hidden past, or dating the earliest stabs at competition, gives little in the way of modern day perspective. Current interest lies in the rowing's formation as a legitimate water-based sport and from there, the unintentional offshoot of indoor rowing as its own sport.

In the early portion of the 18ᵗʰ century, Great Britain (specifically London) would play host to first meager races, which were soon to be mirrored in North America and roughly 100 years later, rightfully situated in the collegiate resting houses of Yale and Harvard. From that point forward and with great thanks to the financial success of these schools, not to mention their lucky placement near suitable water systems, this "newborn" was given enough incubation time for permanency. Despite the growth and acceptance of water-based rowing, the emergence of indoor rowing would be a very long time in the making.

Introduction

Indoor rowing has long lagged behind the advances of its water-born parent. Surprisingly, indoor rowing machines date back well over 100 years, but in these early days and even for generations to come, the engineering would be marked by exceedingly crude designs, along with poor measurement capabilities. Unrefined and cumbersome, they would remain an unattractive option for all but the most stubborn. Indoor rowing, as a sport, would have to wait until 1981, with the release of Concept2's fan-based rower, to see the first truly modernized machine with accurate measurement capabilities. This year would not only mark the beginning of a new sport, but also the birth of a fledgling industry. In the following years, a company by the name of WaterRower would make its mark with an exceedingly distinctive water-based model. It would be these two companies which would win over the hearts and minds of rowing enthusiasts worldwide and would set the stage for what could only be described as a polarity shift; a sport once only respected on water, would now give way to a new land-based competitor. A competitor not only seen as an alternative, but as a unique form of exercise, -having certain advantages over its parent. At the birth of this young and nimble sport, it is doubtful that anybody truly grasped the degree of merit brought forth by these simple machines.

Chapter 1

The People's Choice

For myself, rowing's introduction came about during the college years. The academic atmosphere, while which not completely stifling, gave little in the way of enjoyment. Life outside the classroom wasn't much better and would at times prove itself to be little more than an exercise in futility. In other words, boredom had set in. Joining the rowing team would at least kill some of the monotony. At that point, anything would have served as a welcome change. There were many activities to choose from, but nothing other than rowing had any great appeal. A secondary sport would be perfect, -time displacement was minimal and a little extra fitness never hurt anyone. As with most secondary sports, partaking athletes are generally out-of-shape and a relaxed, non-competitive atmosphere is almost guaranteed. Joining a secondary sports at any given college is just a matter of walking-on and signing-up. In all honesty, the lack of a filtration was more than refreshing. Upon the first team meeting, our coach seemed nice enough and went over the basics. During our next meeting, a somewhat odd statement was made regarding rowers not being your normal types. He went on to say that people on rowing teams are generally high achievers and more often than not, type "A" personalities.

To my great surprise, nobody on the team was out of shape and this came as a bit of a shock; undoubtedly a strange occurrence for a secondary sport! The team was an agreeable bunch and solely focused on getting some time on the water. Our initial practices consisted of getting up at 5:00 am and running at the track building. Without question, part of the rowing game seems involve heavy doses of sleep deprivation. Afternoons consisted of going to the gym for a combination of high repetition weightlifting, along with minor work, such as the abdominal training. After lifting weights, every day would end-out with work on the indoor rowing machines. At college, the set goal for almost all students is to sleep-in as long as possible. While in a sleep deprived state, these three-tiered daily training sessions were akin to torture. Something was real strange here and one thing was for sure, the rugby team sure didn't have this kind of daunting regimentation. For those guys, post training cool-downs consisted of beer and cigarettes.

Indoor rowing machines have gone by many names, but of them

all, the term "torture machine" seems to be most appropriate. Most crew members didn't call them torture machines or indoor rowers, -they were simply referred to as ergs. If not already understood "erg" is an abbreviation for ergometer. We used relatively cheap, but extremely strong wind-resistance models. These machines were crude, loud and came with tank-like durability. You could hammer on them all day long for five straight years and they would still function as new. Despite the noise and lack of aesthetics, these early fan based models had the great advantage blowing air on the athletes. In a sweaty gym, during mid July, they went a long way to keep you cool!

For six straight weeks, the above regimen would be followed. The aquatic realm would be forbidden until proper fitness was attained, along with one little caveat, -proof of swimming ability. Apparently, drowning in the river was against the rules. The swim test was interesting to say the least. Hopeful rowers-to-be were thrown into a pool with two pairs sweat pants and two sweatshirts on. As could be imagined, such water-logging adds a great deal of weight to the body. Had all of us been smarter, 100% cotton-based clothing would not have been the choice du jour. Swim laps for 15 minutes without dying and victory was at hand. We all made it without a hitch. It really wasn't bad from a physical standpoint, but the shock of hitting the cold water after not having swum in ten plus years was a bit of an eye opener.

Keeping with Murphy's Law, problems quickly arose. I would be forced into evening classes due to daytime slots being filled and unfortunately, the evening was when we would be going out on the water. Three practices per week could be made, but missing two or more might prove troublesome. This would turn out to be a major issue! Other problems were also starting to brew.

Our once mellow team members were starting to conflict with the coach about the dauntingly rigorous training schedule, not to mention his combative nature. To many, a training regimen consisting of running in the morning, followed by afternoon erg training/weightlifting and then finalized by evening water-rowing, was at best insane. By this point, our training went from three-tiered to four-tiered and the team was not having it. Most members stopped going to the gym, but always made it for the on-water practices. This type of regimentation is more of what might be seen at larger, more competitively geared Ivy League schools. In all honesty, it is doubtful that most Ivy League schools would have allowed four training sessions per day. This was over training at its worst! Luckily, youth was on my side and without question, an older body would not have been able to handle it. There is something to be said for being young, dumb and tough as nails.

As far as my indoor rowing times went, I somehow managed to exceed what other high-end college level rowers were accomplishing at the time and the coach was somewhat shocked, if not confused by the numbers on the stopwatch. He just looked at it, shook his head and checked it again. He never really said much about it. It's a good thing we didn't use heart rate monitors back then. I don't even want to imagine how high my heart rate was! At times, it was probably nearing 200 beats per minute. The basic idea was just to go as fast as possible. We were told to do 2,000 meters at a full pace and that was about it for instruction. These practice sessions were greatly lacking in any sophisticating and again, the whole idea was to go as fast as possible with a "blood and guts" strategy. Every once in a while, we would take a stab at 5,000 meter races, but those were a rarity.

The effects were almost immediate; my body fat levels dropped faster than I, or anybody else could have possibly imagined. I had never been heavy, but then again, I had never been anywhere close to this lean. I was about as vascular as a human could get and still carried a good amount of muscle. For those wondering, -this level of conditioning was gained while skipping the other workouts. Lifting was being done, but it was very limited in nature. As with the other team members, a reduction in "sessions per day" was eventually undertaken. For the most part, only rowing rowing was being undertaken and the results were freakish. A well muscled body and ripped to the bone! For the vast majority of people, this is the perfect choice of body types, hence the name of the chapter.

In general, the body types of rowers differ from other endurance athletes in that they have more upper body mass and often times, thicker, heavier legs. Personally speaking, having some extra mass in the legs, along with a developed upper body is highly desirable. After all, strong legs, with the addition of an upper body "V" taper is what visually defines the male body. The health effects were far more reaching. I was never tired; I could go all day long without stopping. A strong, lean body with never-ending energy is a combination few could not want. Strange psychological effects were also starting to happen. I was just a little bit happier, but couldn't exactly figure out as to why. Was rowing creating a psychological enhancement, which other sports could not duplicate? I had always been extremely active in sports, but had never managed to reach this level of conditioning; this remained true not only for the physical side, but also the mental.

Rowing on the water is a strange endeavor to say the least. First of all, you're not facing the direction you're going. The Nazi coxswain at the end of the boat is the only one who gets to see much of anything. Coxswains are typically very small, usually weighing in at 100 pounds or so and by way of mandate, come well equipped with strong vocal cords. It is the duty of the cox to set the pace and keep the team motivated. The cox controls the entire boat and their job is a whole lot harder than it looks. Initially, they appear as little more than high-strung cheerleaders and little else. In reality, they are constantly monitoring each rower's stoke to stay in perfect timing and all the while, keeping a keen eye on the other boats for general pacing; their job is a busy one and proficiency only comes with a great deal experience. One of the key requirements for being a cox centers on weight. Typically speaking, short, lean and light is the way go, -with the greatest emphasis being placed on "light." True to form, ours was about five feet tall, weighing in at 92 pounds (soaking wet). As we didn't have speakers in the boat, our cox had ample opportunity to exercise her vocal cords. And yes, he was a she.

Once you're strapped into the footrest, that's it and nothing more can be expected in terms of visual stimulation. You're confined to looking straight ahead at a small section on the rowers back in front of you. You don't get to look around and there is no sightseeing. Pure slavery is a good way to describe it. There is some irony in that a sport so beloved for its beauty, is so completely devoid of visual stimulation for its practitioners. This mandate of forced tunnel vision would seem as a minor annoyance, but it was somehow unusually afflictive. You're little more than a high performance racing piston trying to keep pace with the other engine parts. Rowing at the competitive level is a game of pain tolerance, proper synchronization and the body's ability to utilize oxygen. Of all of these, the ability to withstand pain, is in my opinion, the single most important factor. When athletes first join competitive rowing teams, the typical description of rowing is not that of hard or tough, but rather, as grueling and sadistic. This remains true, even of athletes highly conditioned from previous sports.

I quickly learned there was a big difference between rowing on the ergs and real water-rowing. When rowing on the water, an oar can get stuck in the water in what amounts to a very annoying situation. This holy mess, known as catching a crab, is unknown to most non-rowers. If you're unfamiliar with what a "crab" is, then allow for some explanation. Just as the stroke is finishing, the oar has to be pulled out of the water at a certain angle. If this part is screwed-up, or the oar was placed incorrectly in the first place, the drag of the boat will pull the oar down and keep it there. Keep in mind, the boat is moving pretty fast and the resulting drag is anything but weak. This dragging of the oar is similar to an under-tow effect or what might be described as a parachute effect. However, this is no parachute gently catching the wind, it is incredibly violent by comparison and injuries from the oar swinging back and hitting the rower are not uncommon. I have seen boxing style knockouts, teeth lost and believe it or not, rowers being hit so hard as to fling them right out of the boat. For those avoiding injury, the oar can be righted, but only with a violent tug. By then, you're now out of sync with the other rowers and without question, making the boat shake violently. Rowers have to stay in correct timing for good efficiency and this timing is what keeps the boat well balanced. And of course, a well-balanced boat moves faster through the water than one jiggling side-to-side. This "catching a crab" is a normal mistake for beginners and happens occasionally to the more experienced. That being said, they are a true nightmare for anyone unfortunate enough to experience one! If one is caught, a race is lost.

By now, we were into the season, but practices were still off-and-on due to interfering classes. However, morning running was now replaced rowing practices on the water and these I could always make. By this point, tempers were starting to flair and relations between the coach and the team were steadily deteriorating. I imagine most Ivy League schools get their pick of grade "A" athletes, not to mention, having secondary strings to work with. For our football obsessed college, we were the only eight men in the entire school who signed up. Please allow for a correction to be made. Our original headcount only numbered six, but luckily, a few senior members were able to corral two more in. The team as a whole was not delusional and knew full well the statistical odds overtaking Harvard or Yale.

Given this understanding, team members saw no reason for such incredibly strict and oftentimes abusive discipline. Without missing a beat, the rebelling commenced. The cyclical pattern of team members acting-out, followed by the coach going off on anger infested tirades, would become the mainstay of this rowing clubs early season. As with any pressure cooker, only so much heat can build-up before an explosion occurs.

Memories of just how cold it was during early morning spring practices remain vivid to this day. Anyone who has rowed at colleges occupying more northern latitudes, should have little trouble recalling such occurrences. The discomfort caused by cold temperatures, along with the corresponding adrenaline surge, ingrains memories far past the point of any possible erasure. While trembling in the boat and seeing condensation coming from every breath, questions regarding the payoff, along with preferential thoughts of rowing indoors came to mind with great ease. Today would be one of those days and the early stiffness would prove problematic. We strapped our feet into the scull's footrests and were off. As the boat gained full speed, a crab was caught and not long after, yet another. The response from the coach was swift, -another five minute tirade consisting of every derogatory word in the dictionary. At the time of the incident, our coach was in a low slung power boat 30 plus yards away, -slightly catty-cornered to our position. Despite the distance, the mega-phone made a very close and personal relationship. From this day on, the already stressed relationship would further deteriorate into what could only be described as a black hole. The team became despondent, the coach exasperated and the situation as a whole, completely unwork-able. I would leave the team that day and never look back. The coach would leave the team one week later.

As to why matters between the coach and the team deteriorated so rapidly is debatable. Were the team members' reactions the result of confronting an abusive, power-obsessed coach, or were the coach's tirades an honest retort to a very young and defiant team. The "why" factor is of little concern, however, highlighting the situation is of great importance due its commonness. Group dynamics break down constantly and failures are oftentimes more prevalent than successes. Despite the negativity, great lessons were learned and the advantages of indoor rowing were becoming increasingly clear.

The economics of the water-based rowing didn't make sense. The amount of investment verse the return was horrendous. With complete dedication demanded, little to no joy being had and the odd situation of rowers spending very little time on the water, the activity becomes more of a crucible than a sport. Not to mention, it is a ton of work and time just to get the boat on the water. Where is the payoff? Other sports, while demanding half as much dedication and attention, offer far greater rewards. From this vantage point, rowing on the wa-ter was a bad investment.

If the economics of rowing were not bad enough, the associated problems with group dynamics would prove almost damning. Hu-mans are difficult, -well, very difficult at times. Starting from infancy and throughout adulthood, we are constantly shipped from one group to another. Whether it be school, work, or social activities, -group dynamics are part of societal framework and the good and bad must be dealt with. When in groups, future happiness is entrusted upon the group getting along. THIS IS A DICE ROLL! And with all groups, a director must be present and once again, you will most assuredly receive the honor of being the dancing bear in the circus. Sit, stand, move left, move right, -what a drag.

Past a certain age and level of development, human nature demands self-direction with regard to free time and without such freedom, little more than another indignation is to be had. You should be able to say when, where, for how long, or at the very least, be in agreement with the situational factors. Otherwise, its just another job. And that is just what rowing on the water became, -a very, very bad job. In the end, water rowing went from a sport which I would not recommend due to poor economics, to one, when factoring in group dynamics, would obtain a harsh "avoid at all costs" status. Added together, the two were just too ruinous. Sacrifice and risk are fine, but it has to be worth it.

While the crew-team's gears never turned, time spent on the indoor rower worked out perfectly and "lessons" gained in this sphere proved to be exceedingly positive. Rowing on the erg gave an incredibly sense of enjoyment and accomplishment. It could be done as desired, properly maintained and without question, gave back far more than it took. The physical effects were simply outstanding and these "effects" would prove to be a little mystifying. My early years were exceedingly physical and throughout my upbringing, multiple sports were undertaken at exceedingly high levels of exertion. Anyone with common sense would have expected these sports to produce a level of conditioning at least on par with what indoor rowing offered! After all, what is the difference? Busting your butt at one activity is not all that different from busting your butt at another. In truth, they were not even close and the payoffs from indoor rowing would prove themselves to be greater than anything attained in previous sports. What on earth was going on here?

Such surprising and quick changes would be shrugged off by myself, but wouldn't be lost on others. Repeated comments of "Your ripped to the bone," along with "What the heck are you doing," were seeing increased repetition. Seven percent body fat, packed with muscle and infused with surging vascularity, -tends to be an attention getter; people are attracted to what they want for themselves. I had always been in shape, but nothing really came close to this! Oddly enough, these changes, while vastly out-scoping other exercises, seemingly required little more effort. Regardless of any reality, it just didn't feel harder.

All of this seemed too good to be true and certain questions started coming forth. How could such an unbelievably elevated level of conditioning be achieved with rowing? How could all this be accomplished without injury? How could all this be done without burnout? Again, other sports had been pushed to their maximum limits and attainments such as these had never been seen. Was there was something different about indoor rowing? Without question, I believe the answer is yes and in the following chapters, I will share with you as to why this is the case.

Chapter 2

<u>Perfection In Exercise</u>

Speak with anyone lacking proper knowledge of indoor rowing and it won't be long before interesting comments start spewing forth. Such comments are oftentimes less than favorable and have a tendency to leave indoor rowing enthusiasts a little off balance. It won't be long before they ask as to why such an odd choice would be made. Keep talking, -speak of the benefits of indoor rowing and mention how easily fat is reduced without injury. What you will typically experience is a period of laughter, vexing looks and general bewilderment.

Yes, indoor rowing is oftentimes looked upon as an oddball exercise. Such notions are by no means abnormal and any expectancy

regarding spontaneous understanding is at best naive. For many, rowing conjures up unfashionable images of old-school California gym-
rats wearing headbands, striped tube-socks, along with heavily grown,
sweat soaked, oh-so sweet "lamb-chop" style side-burns. To boot,
early machines had a somewhat goofy and clunky nature. After all, a
multitude of machines were around well before the inception of Con-
cept2's model and still occupy peoples' minds. For those a little
younger, such imagery may not be avalable, but with indoor rowing's
advantages being poorly understood, skepticism and mistrust still pre-
vail. You can't blame people, -they have been lied to all of their
lives! How many infomercials selling junk have they seen. How
many dietary supplements promising near miraculous weight loss
have they seen. How many new-age ministers of hope, happiness
and correct thinking have they seen. The children of the info-mercial
era believe little without proper experimentation. And heck, everybody thinks cardio is cardio and why would anyone use one of those
"strap in" rowing machines when they could just run outside, ride a
bike, jump rope, stair step and/or run on a treadmill. The answers
might be surprising!

So why then is indoor rowing the best exercise? First off, rowing uses all of the major muscles of the body; when comparing rowing to other exercises, most fall short. Long distance runners, for example, primarily use their legs. This results in very sinewy leg
muscles and upper bodies which are hardly visible from the side. I've
always thought the builds of long distance runners were akin to that
of anorexic supermodels. I've seen concentration camp survivors

who had more meat on their bones and without question, looked healthier. Essentially, they have pencil-thin legs and extremely small, underdeveloped chests, which are only more so complemented by their spindly bird arms. Obviously, having such an underdeveloped and withered body is not ascetically pleasing.

Ascetics aside, there is a disturbing lack any real physical strength! This is not a natural state for any fully grown man or wo-men to be in. If runners were using more of their upper bodies to take part of the workload off their legs, they could obviously engage in more intense workouts, for shorter time periods. In this area, rowing surpasses running in a big way. With running, the vast majority of work is being done by the legs. With rowing, the work is split between the upper and lower body. Because of this distribution, it is easier for rowers to do more work for any given amount of time.

For another comparison, take a look at jumping rope. Jumping rope is a good calorie burner, but it mainly uses the calf muscles, with a little of the upper legs. Typically, the calf muscles burn out long before the rest of the body is even tired. As a result, most people have to stop after a very short time, -long before the entire body is even remotely spent. If they were able to spread some the workload from the calves onto other muscles, this exercise would be easier to manage. This also means less localized soreness after exercising due to the workload being distributed over the entire body.

Stair climbing has the same shortfalls. Stair climbing is an ex-cellent exercise and one known for being excruciatingly brutal for those not in tip-top shape. However, the upper body is not utilized to any great degree. Unlike jumping rope, this exercise uses far more of the leg muscles and even hits the butt to some extent. This exercise is certainly better than jumping rope, but still has certain deficiencies. Wouldn't it be easier to endure this exercise if a wee-bit more of the workload were transferred to the upper body? The answer is yes and by utilizing the back and arms, the same number of calories (or more) could be easily burned, with less perceived effort and time.

What about swimming? Swimming is a great exercise. With the exception of possible drowning, nothing bad can really be said about it. Swimming is one of the few exercises which works the entire body with no impact whatsoever. Folks, it does not get any better than this! Swimming also has one amazing attribute which no other exercise can claim. When placed in the water, pressure, by way of uniform compaction, is placed upon the entire circulatory system, which in turn makes it easier for blood to get back to the heart's main pumping chamber. This effect is nearly the same as women wearing support pantyhose, but with the water pressure, far more is given in terms of total coverage. Either way, pressure is being taken off the entire circulatory system and the heart now has an easier time pumping. The end result is less observed fatigue and an incredible situation has been set up where more work can be done without over stressing the heart. An amazing environmental advantage to say the least! Proficiency in any exercise is just as much about the level of heart conditioning as it is about the muscles and lungs. By submerging yourself in water, a little trick has been accomplished which allows for more directly applied muscular effort while decreasing what would normally be the corresponding/required effort of the heart.

Some might wonder why such praise would be given to swimming, when focus is given to indoor rowing. Truthfully speaking, swimming is an amazing exercise and is unfortunately under praised. It is simply unparalleled as a cardio exercise. Swimming has no real faults, but there are faults regarding pools. Lack of them is the first big problem; pools are few and far between. Additionally, pools typically have horrifically high chemical levels that wreak havoc on the hair, skin, eyes and every other part of the body. Unfortunately, swimmers have to inhale the vapors coming off the water and these chemicals do creep into the bloodstream. In northern climates, pools are only open in the summer and just try to find an indoor pool in the winter; they are even fewer and farther between. Not to mention, people in extremely bad shape are oftentimes not too keen on exposing their bodies in tight fitting swimwear. It is truly rare to hear a woman say how excited she is to go swimming and show off her cottage-cheese backside. Most people will avoid such situations at all cost. There are a few people without shame, but luckily, they too are rare. More importantly, for those desiring swimming as an exercise, -lap lanes are needed. Most pools just don't have room for these lanes and if they do, only one person can use an entire lane at a time. Many Olympic swimmers even have trouble finding pools for which lap lanes are consistently available. For an extremely large percentage of the population, consistent cardio exercise via swimming is not a viable option.

Indoor and outdoor bike riding have the same faults as running,

stair climbing and jumping rope. Again, almost all of the work is being done by the legs. If consideration is given to the gross morpho-
logy of bike-endurance athletes, they're not as bad as the runners, but
then again, can it really be said that they're anything other than mar-
ginally better? I've always thought long distance cyclists were built
in a similar fashion to Jurassic Park's raptors. Their legs are fairly
well developed, but their arms are not even that of birds. Again, the
workload should have been split between the upper and lower body
and once again, it's not! To make matters worse, some bikes have a
very nasty problem and this will be spoken of shortly.

Next we need to move onto the the various stand-up exercise
machines, which try to incorporate the arms via some sort of resistance. While never enjoying great popularity, savvy advertising has
allowed for sizable sales. These machines often do not correctly split
the the workload between the upper and lower body. Rowing's seated
position allows for optimal workload distribution. Any exercise in
which you are standing does not distribute the work load in a proper
fashion. Not to mention, some of these machines only work the hip
flexors (swinging/scissor machines) and are of dubious value. Lastly,
these machines do not incorporate the soothing back & forth movement of rowing and as is well known, standing in one place equals a
whole lot of boredom.

I now have a real bone to pick and the yoga/Pilates people are
the guests of honor. Yoga is not even a cardio exercise, but it must be
addressed due to its massive and ever growing popularity. Welcome
to freak-ville, destination zero! My beef is not so much with yoga/Pi-

lates exercises, as it is with the participants themselves, -who at every turn, incessantly slam cardiovascular exercise. Don't get me wrong, yoga and Pilates are wonderful for you and don't let me stop you from partaking in them. Honestly though, so many of these professed freaks have a certain attitude whereby cardio training is cast as a sport for western minds which hurts the body and is akin to a junky's way of relieving stress. This is garbage, -**the human body was designed for cardio fitness**! Take any of these cardio hating converts and ask them to run one mile without stopping and see what happens. I bet they can't do it! It's not hard to assume that being able to run one mile without the fear of having a heart attack is a sign of good health. If you think about it, most children can easily do this, but after years of sedentary lifestyles, most adults can't.

I'm going to let you in on a little secret; most yoga centers don't look like the ones seen on TV and certainly don't look anything like the ones in young n' trendy cities. Many of them are loaded with fat people who are going nowhere fast. As for the instructors, ...well, -they are oftentimes not doing much better. I have seen more than one of them (sometimes very prominent figures) with body fat levels exceeding anything a doctor would recommend as safe. And most of these instructors practice yoga for hours and hours a day! Here is an-other little secret; many "fit" yoga instructors secretly use cardio to stay thin. Yoga is a poor calorie burner to say the least and it meas-ures far less than walking. Now granted, practicing yoga is better than nothing at all, but it irks me when these people start ranting about yoga decreasing cortisol levels and how high cortisol levels increase weight. They will state, with fists in the air, that yoga reduces stress. And as their mantra continues, "Decreased stress from yoga leads to decreased cortisol and decreased cortisol leads to less fat storage." And so on and so on and so...............

Cortisol does have an effect on the storage of fat, but they are missing the point. Excess fat is mainly the result of sedentary lifestyles, not hyper-elevated cortisol levels. Weight gain in relation to elevated cortisol is only of great importance when considering serious illnesses, such as Cushing's syndrome. If you are overweight and betting on standard yoga significantly eliminating body fat via cortisol reduction, -then you are in for a very rude awakening. Simply being happy and relaxed has more to do more with decreasing cortisol than any other single factor. Here is an idea, go buy a rowing machine, lose some weight and see how happy you become as a result. I guarantee that any extra cortisol formerly produced by stress will instantly drop-off as a result of your new-found health. Being happy with what you see in the mirror can have near miraculous effects. If yoga does not address obesity and obesity is one of the leading preventable causes of disease, it's clear that yoga is not the best exercise. Yoga does have benefits, especially when it comes to maintaining healthy, arthritic free joints, but very little when it comes to fat reduction.

Sense of Motion

As mentioned before, swimming has an amazing attribute. Rowing machines have one also. Indoor Rowing is the only machine-based exercise in which the entire body moves back and forth. Why is repetitive horizontal motion so important? This motion somehow stops the exercise from becoming boring. Rowers don't harp on this subject, but everyone who rows knows about it. Rowers know it either consciously or subconsciously, but they do know it! Our mind's enjoyment of this horizontal movement cannot be understated and rowing machines are the only piece of cardiovascular equipment to accomplish this feat. This back and forth horizontal movement not only keeps the boredom away, but also has the peculiar psychological effect of inducing calm states. I call this The Rocking Chair Effect.

Eventually, rowers establish a rhythm and slight trance like state takes over. Please do not misinterpret what is being said here. Rowing's effect is NOT equivalent to a strong altered state of consciousness, nor should it be, but the effect is noticeable, enjoyable and for reasons not fully understood, calming. Again, as to exactly why this enjoyable/relaxing effect happens is unclear. And for those wondering, this effect is not the same as the so-called endorphin rush that runners get. This is something completely separate which is uniquely generated from the back and forth movement.

Surely, there is some brain scientist, somewhere out there, who could put forth some interesting ideas on how the brain processes repetitive horizontal body movement, the stimulation of the central nervous system and its corresponding effects on perception and mood. The truth is, I don't really care. I am just glad this effect occurs. Without this effect, I would not write a book on the benefits on indoor rowing. Most rowers don't think about it much and it's just something taken for granted. Boredom is the number one enemy of exercise equipment. It's not "lack of motivation," but rather, a lack movement which results in boredom. This is why riding bikes outdoors is so popular, but exercising on stationary bikes is mind numbing. Almost everyone who buys stationary bikes abandons them for long periods of time. The body kinetics of the pedaling is roughly the same for both indoor and outdoor bikes, so the linear movement on the street or trail is the only real difference. Trust me, some might say it's the scenery and fresh air, but those are not the major factors. The difference is in the movement!

Some research is pointing to indoor rowers getting more enjoyment out of rowing than other exercises involving "linear" or straight ahead movement. This increased effect may be due to repetitive back and forth motion having a strong effect on the release of the body's own pain killers. The subject matter seems promising, but there is need for more scientific research before anything concrete can be said. Nonetheless, the link between perception, repetitive movement and chemical changes occurring throughout the brain provide for an exceedingly interesting subject matter. Just watch a baby calm down after being rocked and you won't need any more scientific inquiries.

Chapter 3

Avoiding Common Injuries

We see it all the time, football players being led off in stretchers, soccer players with blown ligaments, basketball players with a fully torn achilles tendons and as far as injuries are concerned, professional hockey is a given. All impact sports suffer from the same problems. Abuse of this nature can be justified by professional athletes getting paid millions, but your average "Joe," -thee extraordinary weekend warrior, certainly can't. The idea of exercising is to keep the body fit for a lifetime and not to become a cripple by the age of 40. The best solution is to avoid all impact sports unless serious money is being paid. Sadly, many of these "paid" athletes never fully recover from such injuries and their once perfect bodies start mirroring that of little old ladies. Oh, yes, they're still big, still strong, but remain completely broken in terms of functional usage. Once giants of their chosen sports, acceptance of barely being able to complete daily tasks now has to be given. Sooner or later, people are going to realize how sad it is for athletes, or anyone else for that matter, to be so damaged in their early forties and sometimes long before. Surgical procedures have improved immensely, but problematic occurrences, with regard to surgical errors, even when low, are far too worrisome for most. Even in the case of error-free treatment, problems still exist with the procedures themselves and what is often hoped for as a full restoration, becomes little more than a cheap workaround. For those obtaining good results, post surgical problems are often experienced down the road. Anything from early onset arthritis, to problems with poor alignment, tend to sneak up on those hoping for free n' clear futures. How many times have we heard of people complaining of old war injuries? In most cases, the only real battle occurred on the operating table.

The point here is not not to become overly critical and become a hammer upon the health care system. There have been many success stories and for those, much in the way of adulation is deserving. Victories aside, health care is not perfect and for that reason alone, complete prevention should the first choice for all people, all of the time. When it comes to your health, the dice-roll is never comforting, even when favorable odds are available.

For those already understanding the problem at hand, the natural tendency is to move away from body-to-body impact sports and the natural choice for most is running outdoors (typically light jogging).

Most people figure running to be far safer than any contact sport. And hey, how could anyone get hurt when nobody is trying to tackle you? The disturbing truth is that many runners get far more injuries than even football players. Many experienced long distance runners look as though they've gotten into a knife fight with a dwarf. Their knees have tiny, thin scars from multiple surgeries which look similar to that of a tic-tac-toe board, -albeit one made of scar tissue.

Most would link these problems to weekend warriors pushing too hard and this assumption would be dead wrong. These injuries are the result of daily repetitive stress from hard-core endurance train-ing and not that of overzealous weekend warriors. And the more run-ning is done, the greater the risk. The annals of running history are filled with champions who had to quit at very young ages due to mul-tiple injuries and the odd problem of their legs being shot from over-use. Moreover, it's not uncommon for runners to get hit by cars and occasionally experience the frenzied dog chase. It's fine if the furry-fanged monster coming after you is the neighbor's lazy dog from the kennel, but it's an entirely different story when it's a german shepard or pit bull terrier. Weather is the greater issue and this is especially true for those occupying more northern latitudes. Snow, ice, rain, ex-treme heat, humidity, along with wild fluctuations in temperature all make running difficult to maintain.

If the aforementioned problem of ankle/knee destruction were not bad enough for normal athletes, there are far greater dangers for those packing a few extra pounds. When overweight and doing load bearing exercise (e.g., running), you're not really doing cardio in the same manner as a lighter person. You're doing a dangerous form of hyper-accelerated weightlifting whereby extreme pressure is being place on the heart, joints and muscles. This is not optimal for weight loss and most certainly not maintainable due to the high intensity. Trust me, a heavier built person will either quit from extreme fatigue or serious injury; in no time flat, one or the other will happen! More important than injury is the danger of hyper-elevated heart rates when at high weight levels. An average 150 pounder (in-shape-man) can run a mile without super-elevating his heart rate. Take a 250+ pounder (out-of-shape-man) and have him run that same mile and his heart rate level will be elevated to near maximum danger levels. This can literally translate into a heart attack and sadly, sometimes does. Don't feel bad though! If you took that 150 pound male runner and stuck 100 extra pounds on his back, it wouldn't be long before he too collapsed. Some arrogant athletes never seem to understand the math when it comes to such situations.

Most heavy weight athletes who are privy to the problem will often choose moderate walking until they get in-shape or at least some of the weight off. Walking is excellent for relaxation and has the added benefit of increasing circulation. Without question, walking is certainly better than doing nothing, but not by much. The problem with walking is its poor calorie burning. Walking does not burn all that many more calories than simply standing (upright) and doing nothing. More than any other activity, the human body was designed to walk. As a result of our wonderfully engineered skeletal system, while walking, most of the work load is transferred to the bones. The incredibly efficient bio-mechanics of the human body creates perfect balance from one step to the next. Throughout each step, the majority of weight is kept perfectly centered over the skeletal system and by design, large musculature is **not** overly activated. People can often walk for extremely long distances with minimal fatigue. This highly optimized effort-to-output is a wonderful testament to the design of the human body, but again, such built-in "economy" results in poor calorie burning. You would have to walk for a couple of hours a day to see good fat burning effects. The only real way to do this is to have a job where you work on your feet all day. Running, on the other hand, is a great fat burner. Running takes the body out of its effort-saving movement and transfers more of the weight to the muscles. It also transfers more stress to the joints and as we all know, major problems are created from this fact alone. In the end, long distance running is not safe for lean people and is extremely dangerous for those with larger body types. Running is out, as is walking! That being said, walking is not to be totally dismissed. It does work to some degree and serves as a safer alternative to running, but there are better options.

Bike riding, as in Tour de France style, is generally the other "go-to" cardio sport for men and women wanting to avoid contact sports. Bike riding is perhaps the most dangerous of them all! When riding bikes, you have to go extremely long distances and generally, the only way to do this is by staying on the roads. Unfortunately, roads are filled with cars, or fast moving "Death Rams" as I like to call them. If you ride a bike for any major amount of time, taking a very bad all is almost guaranteed. The main crux of the problem lies not so much with the spill itself, but the multi-thousand pound cars which are soon to be colliding with you. Some serious tragedies have happened for both the motorists and the bikers. Many professional cyclists have funny, if not frightening stories concerning various close calls with vehicles. They will often speak freely of being scared out of their minds and pushing safety limits far beyond the "safe zone" of common sense. Apparently, in many parts of the United States, it's a bit of a sport to run bikers off the road. If the professionals have had such troubles, it's a pretty good indication for the rest of us to take note.

Aside from the very real danger aspect, bike riding has a horrid problem which was previously alluded to. In this case, the trouble re-volves around the little plastic seats which are shaped in a similar fashion to the heads of bottlenose dolphins. For years, many bikers suffered silently with impotence and this was a fact which outsiders never caught wind of. It would seem that bikers were somewhat si-lent on the topic! The riders' tight-lipped tendencies were of little sur-prise considering the private nature of the problem; the corresponding embarrassment factor was obviously high. When this issue was bravely spoken of, industry officials and doctors alike quickly releg-ated it as myth. The so-called experts had their say, but the aforemen-tioned sexual dysfunction was no myth and mounting evidence would soon be too great to ignore.

With time and a building of courage, a few more bikers would come forward and these brave few would usher in an industry-wide shock-wave of confessions. Ever increasing numbers of male bike riders fully admitted to complete impotence, along with other complaints such as decreased sexual interest. After nailing things down, all eyes turned toward the seat. When riding in a forward position and especially when cornering, the biker's weight is pressing down on the front-end of the slender bottlenose seat. Essentially, a massive amount of rider's weight is resting on a three inch peg. The area taking much of the brunt is called the perineum. Once this area is repeatedly pressed on too hard, the blood vessels are crimped, eventually damaged and the circulation to the crotch is dramatically reduced. The damaged vessels, horribly enough, are the same ones responsible for feeding the testicles and penis with fresh blood. Lacking any great surprise, riders had also complained about crotch numbness and testicular pain. From here, it does not take a genius to understand the aftereffect. The end result is castration via reduced blood flow!

When I was a child or eight or nine years, my father purchased an ultra-light weight Italian racing bike. I never saw him ride it, not even once. A few years back, I asked him about it and he just smiled. I asked again if he rode it when he was younger (during the period of my childhood). He said he only rode a couple of times and each time his crotch became numb. My father was one of the lucky ones. Low blood pressure runs in our family and this simple fact probably saved him. Someone with higher blood pressure may not have experienced numbness quite as fast. I really don't know if my father understood the inherent dangers of such numbness, but it did spook him enough to stop riding. Even he had the common sense to understand that numbness equals zero blood flow and zero blood flow equals nothing good. That would mark the end of the ultra-sleek Italian racing bike.

Why it took so long to identify this problem is easy to see. One thing men will almost never talk about is the inability to get an erection. If prodded, men will eventually talk about personal tragedies, their feelings, but will almost never talk about erectile dysfunction or a lack of sexual interest. It seems that men tend to link their identity as a "man" to their libido and the functioning therein. As an added irritation, industry officials have been understating and downplaying the problem for years. After all, not everybody gets this problem. Well, -that is true! Not everybody who smokes gets cancer and not everybody who uses hard drugs overdoses. What we do know is that these seats are a major problem, just as smoking and drug use are. Problems also exist with proper statistical documentation regarding those experiencing sexual dysfunction resulting from bottlenose seat designs. Cyclists, although braver than before, still remain reluctant to talk about the problem and obtaining legitimate statistics is almost impossible. The next and not so obvious question is whether these "seat problems" are occurring in women. Being that women can't get erections, little in the way of a warning flag is available. Are women also suffering from sexual problems due to poor seat designs? While the ovaries are placed differently testicles, the areas creating sensation are fed by the same vessels. These are matters in need of more research, -unbiased research.

In the last couple of years, much has been done to improve seats for riders. They have come out with seats that don't have the front bottlenose and only allow the rider's weight to be placed on butt. These newer seats do a better job and in some cases, eliminate all of the pressure on the perineum. There are also other seat models which cut-off the top ridge of the bottlenose, thereby placing the pressure on the sides of the rider's crotch and not directly onto the perineum. The odd thing is, current day riders still opt for the same old-style seats and preferentially do so, despite the dangers. When they changed the seat design, they decreased the functionality and riders were not having it. Apparently, what's good for the perineum is not good for racing. This problem is a very long way from being solved. I know we have all enjoyed the superheros of cycling, but advisements for people to stay away from these bottlenose seat designs stay intact.

As to why so much emphasis was placed on arguments against bike riding and running is easy to see. Both work extremely well as a cardiovascular exercises and produce excellent fat loss results. If you look at the athletes in both of these sports, it's obvious they are extremely lean, but at what cost? What good is running if you constantly have to stop doing it because of injuries? Some have even had to stop running for life due to serious knee and ankle injuries resulting from repetitive damage. What good is bike riding if you have to spend one month in a hospital as a result of your first high speed wreck and finally get killed by some idiot chatting-it-up on a cell phone during your second. Between multiple injuries, accidents, gaunt supermodel builds and aforementioned loss of erections/sex drive, participation in these sports is ill advised. There has to be a better way to win at this game!

In comes the rowing machine. With rowing, effort is correctly split between the upper and lower body. As a result, greater levels of effort can be sustained for any given time and you'll never have to worry about a trucker running you off the road. More importantly, you will be able to exercise for less time and gain far better results. This can only be accomplished by virtue of the workload being split between the upper and lower body.

A miracle, absolutely not, -its simple workload distribution. Heavy people can now exercise without joint destruction and more importantly, without fear of hyper-elevated heart rates. Indoor rowing results in the upper and lower body being equally developed. You'll never again have to put up with rain, snow and other outdoor hazards. Lighter weight athletes finally have a sport which eliminates repetitive strike injuries. Happily, this is an exercise with almost no concern for clothing; rowing is very simple in this regard! The burden of expensive gym memberships is a thing of the past and in the time it takes to get ready for the gym, the workout will be finished. Does this sound like an info-mercial? It's not and keep in mind, I'm not hocking any junk exercise equipment. Unlike all the TV salesmen who rant and lie about the latest breakthrough exercise gadget or training system, the expressed virtues of indoor rowing are absolutely true! Still yet, problems and arguments arise.

A Word about the Beef

When picking correct methodologies for fat reduction, modern experts tend to resemble diabolically opposed political camps, more than honest scientists going about their business. It would seem as though a line has been drawn in the sand. With those supporting ultra-long endurance exercises, -the " Zone" motto (in reference to fat burning zones in endurance exercise) is brought forth and with those favoring the heavily muscled style of bodybuilders, -the "Beef Burns Fat" creed reins supreme. Nowadays, the "Beef Burns Fat" creed has steadily crept up in popularity and this mainstay of enhanced muscularity has had no problems hanging on. And this remains true, even as the Hulk-like figures have diminished in favor of more naturally sized, symmetrical builds.

This relatively new theory, heavily supported by clean and factual data, has had little problem gaining general acceptance and scientists now overwhelmingly support the idea of adding additional muscle as a way to enhance the burning of calories. Muscle tissue, just as any other type of cell, requires fuel for survival. The idea here is simple; just add more muscle and astonishingly enough, more calories are burned. Muscle burns calories even when inactive and must do so to stay alive! For the muscle junkies, this revelation offered a level of authentication for a dishonored sport, so shamelessly infested with drugs. The prime directive of this ideology is to gain as much muscle possible and let the extra beef burn away the pounds when inactive.

An interesting and factually backed theory, but why is it then, that so many power lifters are pushing such high body fat levels? After all, power lifters are generally considered to be the most muscular athletes on earth. Now granted, not all of them are carrying such high body fat levels, but a relatively high percentage are! Look at football linebackers, -these boys are carrying more muscle mass than most humans could ever want or even justify and yet, some still have massive pot bellies. The point here is to not get involved with any argument against added muscle burning calories, but simply to place emphasis on the science community missing something. Again, direct arguments against the "calorie burning potential of added muscle" will not be made, but the degree to which the extra muscle ushers-in that change will be challenged. There are a few ideas supporting this contention of "overstatement" and just for fun, one will be addressed, along with one compounding problem.

One of the oddest effects of high intensity weightlifting is its almost unbelievable ability to stimulate the hunger mechanism. This is not normal hunger! More rightfully stated, this is the "I'm going to eat everything in the fridge and come back for another gigantic snack an hour later," type of hunger. My personal experiences during college gave credence to this somewhat undefined, but well understood "hunger response" to weightlifting. When engaging in INTENSE weightlifting, if meals are not taken every 2-3 hours, participants become famished, to the point of feeling starved. This hunger takes hold quickly and has a tendency to override all other objectives; in other words, it just can't be ignored.

My early days of weightlifting made for a body demanding of high calorie levels. Despite gaining large amounts of muscle, being ripped-to-the-bone was little more than a fantasy. Was such overzealous eating cancelling out any increased calorie expenditure from the newly gained muscle? The answer was yes; the muscle burns fat advocates were definitely missing this point. I had a ton of muscle and unfortunately, -the body fat level of a whale before migration. And one other thing, three to four miles of walking was taking place on a daily basis! Not exactly sedentary, now is it? Far too many people are following this cycle of gaining large amounts of muscle and retaining body fat levels far too high for even the remote consideration of six-pack visibility. For myself, proper fat loss would not be obtained until consistent rowing was applied.

In addition to the problem of excessive hunger stimulation, extremely muscular bodies (power lifters, linebackers, professional bodybuilders) may not be the healthiest. All that muscle has to be fed by red blood cells. You better believe all this beef puts extra strain not only on the body to make red blood cells, but also the heart to pump blood throughout the newly formed muscle tissue. Yes, in this case, extra muscle mass is the issue and not the fat. You always hear people talking about how muscle is the good guy and fat being the nasty villain, but there is a point of diminishing returns when it comes to excess bulk. After exceeding some point of muscularity, it's not really about diminishing returns, but rather, negative returns. Ask extremely muscular men how well the sleep. Ask them how tired they are at the end of the day. The answers are rarely good. There is a reason why small dogs live longer than large ones! It would be wise to take this little hint from the animal kingdom!

A Word about Cross-Training

Come one, come all, -how many fitness experts have we heard

chanting about the benefits of cross-training. The main thrust of this "cross-training ideal" revolves around well-roundness in training and its supposed benefits. After all, it is good to be well rounded, but the sad truth is that cross-training often leads to well rounded bellies and thick thighs. Our goal is cardiovascular conditioning/weight loss and not being able to engage in multiple exercises at what I consider to be a low level. People inevitably do these "multiple exercises" at a decreased level of intensity and never fully master any of them. What exactly did they expect to happen? Cross-training practitioners are not properly conditioned for any given exercise and people expect them to perform at an intensity level required for fat loss. Folks, this is a little more than just questionable.

There is a secondary, or by some measures, a primary reason as to why most experts claim cross-training to be advantageous; adherents state that the body becomes acclimated to certain exercises and will no longer burn as many calories as it did when first engaging in the exercise; initially, the body's physical movements will not be conditioned for any given exercise lacking familiarity. As a result, and for lack of a better description, your muscles will be sloppy in the movement. By consequence, the body recruits more muscle fibers during the initial stages of the exercise than it would after many months of repeated practice. More muscle fiber recruitment equals more calories burned and in the end, greater fat loss. And with this great revelation came the theory of cross-training. Just keep shocking and confusing the body and you're bound to get maximum muscle fiber recruitment and thus, -the maximum number of calories burned.

If pondered, it does make sense and legions of people are following this new dogma. This cross-training theory seems to work on paper, but then again, so does communism.

If this claimed detrimental adaptation effect (decreased calorie burning over repeated exposure to an exercise) were as strong as suggested, then endurance athletes only doing one exercise would not be nearly as lean as they are. As mention before, the ill-fated science nerds have missed the larger issue. As with any exercise, it takes the body weeks, if not months to build up proper endurance/strength to sustain the activity long enough, or at a high enough level of intensity to efficiently burn fat. This development only comes through daily or almost bi-daily sustained training in a singular activity.

If a long distance runner tried to ride a bike, he or she would be extremely sore for the next couple of days and would inevitably do poorly. Even though the runner was in terrific shape, his or her muscles were not accustomed to the biking movement and yes, even they will experience soreness. This is not desirable! Extreme pain from exercise should be avoided by repeated conditioning and this repeated conditioning can only be done through singular exercise adherence. If you keep doing differing exercises to which the body is unfamiliar, you're going to be in pain and there is absolutely no way around it. If you are too sore to walk comfortably in morning, then you are obviously too sore to keep exercising. This is what always happens with cross-training! The end result is failure in all exercises and ultimately, your valuable time being wasted. Lastly, people want to stick with one thing and master it. This is the way humans are psychologically wired and it will never change.

Chapter 4

Discovering Strength Endurance

Old Age Way Too Young

Looking back on the careers of many famous marathon runners, we can see the same old story occurring time and time again. Marathon runner "X," who is genetically gifted for the sport, runs non-stop for well over a decade and puts forth incredible performances. Everything is going swimmingly and this little energizer bunny seems unstoppable. Then, with little or no warning, in his or her late twenties or early thirties, something goes terribly wrong.

These runners often start succumbing to knee, ankle and foot injuries which start to spell the end of the road. Endurance athletes are frailer than most people would assume; they get hurt very easily and heal extremely slowly. This slow healing time is itself a warning sign which few endurance athletes ever give proper attention. A bad combination to say the least, but more importantly, a direct signaling of a depleted/non-healthy state being at hand. Without question, an alarming situation and one which oftentimes has far greater consequences than would be expected. What follows is truly a nightmare!

Runner's legs simply start to wear out from years and years of running. The depleted state makes way not only for injuries, but also increased wear n' tear on the micro-level. People in the fitness community refer to this as running on old legs or what I call the old legs problem. It's one thing to get an injury, but quite a different story to have your muscles, joints and tendons clearly shot from years of repetitive strain. Yes, "shot" as in an old set of tires.

Once this phenomenon occurs, nothing much can improve the situation. Runners can often keep running, but never at a level even remotely close to their old glory days. The fact of this happening is not entirely surprising, nor is it unusual in terms of frequency. The unusual part deals more with this "old legs" problem unfolding at such young ages. Many people will attribute this problem to general aging and the normal declines seen therein. People will often say "You're over 30 now, so your body is just slowing down." These statements are nothing more than verbal garbage and any age related declines would result in times which were only slightly lower. These runners are facing time declines which could more accurately be described as falling off a cliff. I never believed this aging explanation! These problems are the result of years of abuse without allowing for substantial recovery time. And again, it's a sign of the human body not being designed to tolerate 60+ minutes of slow paced endurance routines each and every day.

These athletes often feel indestructible in their late teens and early twenties. No pain = no gain! They never think to take time off. And more often than not, they never have any desire to rest. Whether it be running, tennis, or whatever else, these activities have an addiction quality and practitioners strongly identify with their chosen sport. Taking periods of time off would almost amount to a form of mutiny, if not outright withdrawal symptoms.

Some might argue this "old leg" problem to be the result of pounding incurred during load-bearing exercises. This is part of the problem and does in fact lead to many injuries. However, the main problem is one of accumulated micro-damage brought about by the sheer length of the training, which is further aggravated by an inadequate ability to recover. Don't misunderstand the situation, the pounding does cause problems, but the main crux of the problem lies with overuse (extremely high repetitions) and not the pounding itself. This exceedingly high repetition rate, along with the lack of recovery time, leads to poor body chemistry for healing. From there, the process spirals downward with great velocity.

Again, this "old legs" problem is not necessarily the result of repeated impact and does happen to people NOT engaging in load bearing exercises. The best possible example of this would be swimming. Competitive swimmers obviously do not have to put up with the extra pounding which hounds other athletes, such as runners. However, there have been highly competitive swimmers who dominated, to the point of being awe inspiring and then, in their early twenties, just fell-off in terms of competitive times. Their bodies were now ancient from the non-stop abuse and reached the point of no-return. Being 22, 23, or 24 years is not old, nor is there any age related decline at such numbers. More often than not, they were not engaging in normal training, even for competitive athletes! They were pushing training times past what it means to be human and they paid the price for such obsessiveness.

People Without this Problem

The severity of the "old legs" problem is more than clear. There are no magic cures and certainly no quick fixes for this predicament. To find a solution, it would be wise to look for athletes who do not suffer from this problem or at least in athletes where it is minimized.

As luck would have it, there is one group of athletes who are not overly affected by this "old legs" problem. Sprinters have shown an unusual ability to keep sprinting even into their forties and sometimes, -close to fifty or so. It's not so remarkable that they can run, but rather, their ability to keep pace with the younger athletes. There have been cases of runners in their forties absolutely crushing all the "twenty-somethings" with whom they competed. Their names will not be listed, but one or two should easily come to mind. Full acknowledgment is given to sprinting's elite core being mainly comprised of younger athletes. However, it is unusual for such a high number of older adults to have successfully competed against younger athletes in this arena. Given the aggressive nature of sprinting, such an outcome would never be expected. After all, sprinting is a little more hardcore than other sporting activities. The sprinters legs are not wearing out as much as would be expected.

Sprinters have interesting body types. They have muscular legs, somewhat large upper body musculature and fairly low body fat levels. Nothing bad can really be said about their body types. Ascetics are a matter of taste and as most standards have it, sprinters are exceeding well developed. That being said, sprinters may not be perfect, but they are very close.

The interesting question to be asked is exactly how sprinters have such low body fat levels. Modern wisdom states there must be a minimum of 30+ minutes (typically 60) of straight endurance exercise to result in any fat loss at all. Were these athletes just genetically gifted with low body fat levels? Interestingly enough, sprinters are not known for extreme dieting. They deprive themselves very little and workout times are generally short! And yet, they still have eight percent body fat. Truth be told, an hour of cardio (per day) is not needed and this will be addressed in the next chapter. For now, the fact of these athletes having extremely low body fat levels and a good amount of muscle can be agreed upon.

We have found an exercise that achieves our fitness goals. Low body fat levels, a healthy heart/lungs, abundant muscle-mass and a largely absent "old legs" problem is a great combination to say the least. These athletes can't run long distances very well, but heck, we are not interested in extremely long distance exercises! And by the way, sprinting does a far better job at conditioning the heart and lungs than most would think.

As to why sprinters don't seem to suffer from "old legs" problem has to do with their training times. The nature of sprinting is such that "massive amounts per day" cannot be undertaken. Sprinters simply become too fatigued after a couple of runs and putting forth additional effort becomes counterproductive. The idea is to do more work for a shorter period of time. Very short practices along with time set aside for specialty training and that's it! Because these workouts are short (in terms of total running time), the body has time to recover. Bingo, no "old legs" problem and one major block of the puzzle has been completed.

As is typical, with one question being answered, another issue rears its head. Obviously, ultra-long distance training is not necessary for low body fat levels. Sprinting however, at least by way of running, is very problematic. It works well for fat loss, manages to avoid the "old legs" problem, retains muscle mass, but there are problems when it comes to acute injuries. Sprinters have one of the worst records for acute injuries. It's a constant game of getting hurt and having to take time off.

With many sports, athletes get injured now and then, but it's relatively rare to see them constantly going down during competition. Now granted, there are some sports, such as hockey and football, in which competitors are routinely getting battered, but these comparisons works poorly with regard to HOW the injuries are occurring. Sprinters are not getting injured because of player-to-player impact, but rather, from massive amounts of self applied pressure to muscles, joints and tendons. They are constantly dropping with knee problems, severely torn muscles/ligaments and repeatedly reinstating old injuries into new ones, -which in almost all cases, prove themselves to be worse than the originals. This can easily demonstrate how hardcore Olympic level sprinting really can be. Obviously, any athlete better be getting paid to do this, otherwise, it's just not worth it. Sprinting seems to have conquered the "old legs" problem, but has gained the horrific reputation for instilling more acute injuries. Not to mention, it is impossible for your everyday "Joe," with high body fat levels, to exercise via land-sprinting; poor "Joe" will end up hurting himself in no time flat. In the end, sprinting has eliminated the "old legs" problem, but a snag has been caught with the more acute injures. Not to worry, rowing solves all of these problems!

Where Does Rowing Fit In

Many other exercises have been discussed, but very little information has been given on rowing. So what exactly makes rowing different from all of these? Rowing is a strength endurance exercise. Strength endurance is not a common term simply because very few sports or exercises accommodate its definition. Rowing at a fairly intense pace is more demanding than long distance running, regular biking, or casual swimming. It is however, less intense than full out Olympic level short sprints for most disciplines. Strength endurance occupies a clever niche between the two.

Unlike running or biking, people using indoor rowing machines usually never train for more than 30 minutes. Generally speaking, 20 minutes or so seems to be the average for most. There are those who perform marathon races on indoor rowing machines, but these distances have never seen great acceptance. I'm not a big fan of marathon rowing due to the aforementioned "old legs" problem and this is specifically why I instruct people to avoid it like the plague. Generally speaking, 20 minutes is all that it takes and even greater results can be achieved by utilizing shorter time periods, along with correct training systems. Indoor rowing gives an advantage like no other; there is no impact, the legs are used in a tandem position (highly strengthened) and a large percentage of body-weight goes into the seat. As a result, there is little need to worry about acute injuries. Injuries are further reduced by splitting the workload between the upper and lower body; no one part of the body takes all the brunt! This simple advantage keeps YOU from having to go to the doctor and experiencing the joy of getting a knee scoped out, or worse yet, surgically restructured. The advantages regarding injury prevention are by no means trivial! With injuries out of the way, full focus can be given to conditioning. The end result is the upper and lower body developing in a balanced manner, which leads to a state of perfect symmetry. And have no doubt, it is this symmetry which leads to beauty. Furthering the benefits, indoor rowing allows for increased intensity, but without the worriment of ripped muscles and tendons. To sum it up, indoor rowing largely eliminates acute injuries, while at the same time, manages to sidestep the "old legs" problem. Due to the short workout times, plenty of time is left for recuperation. Aside from avoiding the two biggest pitfalls of modern exercise, rowing has the great boon of retaining muscle mass, while simultaneously controlling body fat. And regarding the latter, that's "RIPPED THE BONE" control of body fat. What more could anybody ask for?

Chapter 5

<u>The Cheapest Exercise</u>

At this point, purchasing a rowing machine should come into focus. For most, rowing's introduction will come by way of the erg at the local gym. Yes, it's a good place to start, but recommendations for staying with gyms cannot be made. I personally don't care for them and to be very honest, I detest them. While working out in a small gym during my university days, a fungal infection was unfortunately caught, which led to a very uncomfortable couple of days of having my skin feel as though it was on fire. Only with the aid of some hydrocortisone was this little monster placed under control. That was the last time I went to that particular gym and consequently, why indoor rowing came to an end at college. A few years after college, I joined another local gym and somehow managed, -YET

AGAIN, to get another fungal infection. The first one was bad, but this felt as if the dreaded flesh-eating bacteria had been contracted. Further elaboration won't be given, -as I'm sure you get the idea. Having never been predisposed to such afflictions outside of the gym, no doubt was given to their origin. These infections are almost impossible to stop and gym owners, no matter how diligent at cleaning the machines with anti-"whatever" spray, never really seem to stop their spread. And in this day and age, people have more to worry about than just simple fungal infections. The emergence of new and frightfully powerful bacterial and viral strains are disconcerting to say the least. Based on what has already been seen, concern is beyond validation.

Risk of contracting bugs is not the not the only reason for hating gyms. The normal complaints are all too common and unfortunately valid. Having to waste time driving, getting set-up and waiting for people to get off the various machines is a drag. Not to mention, gyms play host to some of the most unhinged and frenzied personality types in existence. Gyms can be looked at as meeting houses for the neurotically minded. Some of the things I've heard and seen in hard-core gyms goes beyond description. Ultimately, buying a rowing machine is your best bet in the long run. People often have reservations about the price, but this is one point which always brings laughter. Rowing is the cheapest exercise in existence.

A typical pro-level rowing machine will cost anywhere from $900 to a little over 2,000 dollars, with the 1,000 dollar mark being the norm. For those well off, no pain is to be had, but for those on

strict budgets, it's an investment. Even in cases of financially secur-
ity, spending so much money on a piece of exercise equipment can be
troubling. Heck, a medium sized HDTV could be purchased for the
same price. Allow for one great assurance to be given; more TV is
not the answer, -it's the problem.

Take these prices (various rowing machines) and compare them
to the cost of a gym membership. In the short run, the gym membership will be cheaper, but in the long run, the cost will easily exceed
that of a single rowing machine. And the reference to a "long run"
really speaks poorly of the time frame in this situation. In the vast
majority of financial matters, the long run typically signifies 20 years
or more. In our case, the long run equates to two or three year max.
If living in a large city with trendy gyms, one six month membership
could easily cost over 500 dollars and in some of the exceedingly
ritzy areas, thousands upon thousands can be spent.

As should not go unnoticed, most pro-level rowing machines are
built to last a lifetime. At the very least, most professional rowing
machines will give twenty years worth of workouts with very limited
maintenance. Now that is refreshing. Compare that to the upkeep
needed for a treadmill, or better yet, the cost of twenty years worth of
gym memberships. My personal rowing machine is going on nine
years and not a single repair has been made to it, nor any maintenance. Everything works exactly as it did from the date of the machine's first row!

Compare the cost of indoor rowing to that of golf, soccer,
hockey, tennis, football, baseball, or just about any other sport ima

ginable and the differences will be staggering. All of these sports require expensive gear and traveling expenses. Adding weight to the argument, very few of these traditional sports can be played in bad weather. The poor weather conditions in any location are of little concern. There is no need to worry, you'll be rowing all winter long. When exercising for health, consistency is needed and not some on-again/off-again sport played for three months out of the year.

Some might wonder about a far simpler sport such as basketball. Is there any possibility of basketball being more expensive than rowing? Basketball looks very cheap on the surface. Obviously, very little in need in terms of equipment and almost all courts are free of charge. Let's break down the costs and take a closer look.

Basketballs typically range from 7-30 dollars. If playing a great deal, you're going to have to buy a couple a year. Some will just wear out, others will get punctured, run over, or suffer other calamities. For a high use player, four per year will be designated. Basketball shoes are obviously needed and here is where the real problem comes in. Due to ridiculously lavish endorsement contracts, basketball shoes are far more expensive than running shoes. Typically, basketball shoes range from 80-150 dollars, -with the 150 dollar mark being more of the norm. Just to be fair, the average shoe price will be set at 115 dollars and the assumption of a "high use" player going through a pair every two months will be made. Yes, those playing a great deal will easily burn through a pair every two months. Yearly travel expenses have to be added in, -and 50 dollars will be set as the average. Not everyone needs to travel, but still yet, this average remains on the low side. So let's see where we stand.

Basketballs = $19(average cost) x 4 per year   = 76
Shoes   = $115 x 6 per year   = 690
gas/travel   =50

Grand total =$816 per year.

Multiply this by ten years and you get a whopping 8, 160 dollars. Not exactly cheap, is it? In the span of a little over one year, enough money could have been saved for a rowing machine and keep in mind, the rowing machine is only being payed for once. And again, any professional level rowing machine should last a minimum of twenty years. In reality, rowing machines can and do last much longer, but for the sake of argument, twenty will serve as the mark. As for shoes with a rowing machine, ...well, they can take years to wear out. In my opinion, the best shoes for indoor rowing are very light indoor soccer shoes or those designed martial arts. If you search around (cough, cough, amazon.com), they can be gotten on the cheap. Cheap as in 15-20 dollars.

Let's take another example, but this time, the challenge will be more difficult. What is the most simplistic sport in terms of equipment? Running would have to be the number one choice. At its most basic level, shoes are all that is really needed, along with some athletic clothing. Athletes who use running as their main exercise will have to replace their shoes about every month. Letting shoes go any longer can be dangerous due to cushioning loss. All serious runners know to replace their shoes long before the soles are worn out. If running shoes are not frequently replaced, time spent in the sport will be dramatically reduced. Just for fun, a little more difficulty will be applied to this scenario. Most high end running shoes cost anywhere from 100-130 dollars. Let's just say our runner shops around for great deals and gets his or her shoes for 70 bucks a pop.

Running shoes 70 dollars x 12 = 840

Yep, that's 840 bucks a year for just running alone and additional costs for clothing are not included. Again, with some simple math, we can see the price easily going above 8,000 dollars in ten years. Most people would tell you to never buy an expensive rowing machine and just do something cheap. Cheap as in running or basketball! This "nickel and dimming" effect is incredibly misleading and most people never see it coming. Because a rowing machine is only payed for once, the longer it lasts, the cheaper its cost per year becomes. As mathematically obvious as the situation may be, few ever give it proper consideration. Let's say a WaterRower was purchased for a little over 1,000 dollars. After the first ten years, the owner will have only payed a little over 100 dollars a year for it. Not even stingy man, -not even Scrooge himself, could call that a bad deal. Actually, with a longer life expectancy, the cost per year would be lower.

The previous two examples are probably the cheapest sports in existence. Take a minute to consider really expensive sports such as golf, football, hockey and the like. These can easily cost thousands of dollars per year, with golf being the worst offender in this category. For a machine which is almost indestructible and lasts a lifetime, the pricing can't be beat. Rowing's economics are almost unbelievable.

Chapter 6

Rowing's Two Workhorses

With the financial matters being understood, now is a perfect time to take a fun look at rowing's two workhorses. I will take you through an honest review of rowing's two elite machines and go over their various ups and downs. You will be able to get an unbiased opinion and get an idea as to which machine will best suit your needs. Both of these machines are fairly simple in design. Complicated Swiss watches they are not, but the engineering between the two couldn't be any more different. An overview is definitely in order. But before we start, I would like to explicitly state:

That I have no ties to any rowing machine companies/sellers in any way. I do not receive free equipment from manufacturers/sellers nor have I ever taken any money/gifts from manufacturers or sellers. I also am completely devoid of any personal/professional relationships with anyone associated with the manufacturing/sale of any rowing equipment. I have never in the past, nor am I currently investing in any rowing machine companies or sellers. Lastly, I am not working, nor have worked for any manufacturing or sales company associated rowing machines.

In other words, I have absolutely no ties to the rowing industry whatsoever. The two machines being reviewed were chosen by the rowing community and not by myself. Ask enough rowers which machines they prefer and the regularity of hearing the words "Concept2" and "WaterRower" may be surprising. By a coin flip, Concept2 starts us off.

Concept2 Model D (Wind-Based Model)

Our first selection is what may be the most widely used rowing machine on the planet. The Concept2 is an elegant machine and comes with a well-earned reputation for being tough as nails. The Concept2 is the workaholic of the rowing word. Overall, the Concept2 model D has a sleek design, somewhat artful looks, -with functionality being the foremost design principle when it comes to this icon of the rowing world. Concept2 has made its mark on the rowing world by coupling low prices with extreme longevity. To put it simply, the concept2 is nearly indestructible. At the time of this writing, the machine costs 900 dolloars (w/ PM3 monitor). For those desiring more functionality, upgrading to the newer PM4 monitor (+ $150) can be done.

With the Concept2, a lot of machine can be gotten for a very reasonable price, but this alone does account for Concept2's popularity. The Concept2 machines are especially noted for their out-of-the-box calibration. They serve as the measuring stick for almost all worldwide competition. Rowers far and wide trust these machines for accurate time comparisons across the gym and across the world. As would be expected, all monitor information can be uploaded to a PC and compared across the net. The end result is a machine which has become known as the be-all and end-all for large scale competitions. Almost all competitive rowers use Concept2 rowing machines due to their accurate measurement and this "accuracy" is what their reputation has been built on. As with all modern rowing machines, a heart rate monitor can be used with the Concept2 and as would be expected, the built in monitors give a good assortment of workout routines, along with distances, paces, splits and every other metrical bell n' whistle. As indoor rowing has evolved into a competitive sport, there has been a need for a machine to give highly accurate and consistent measurements across all manufactured units in production. For competitive purposes, the Concept2 rowing machine has surfaced as the people's number one choice.

The Concept2 model D has forgone any trickery in the design of its resistance mechanism. The rower utilizes a simple fan design. The harder you pull, the more resistance you get. Every resistance mechanism has its own problems, but this time tested design, although simple, works to near perfection. Sometimes "simple" is good and when it comes to mechanical engineering, this old adage remains true. Working in conjunction with the fan is the damper setting. This "damper" works in a similar fashion to "gearing" and allows differing athletes to set the machine up to best suite their strengths. The damper is a little spoken of feature, which has enormously impacted the success of the Concept2 machine in the competitive sphere.

The Model D receives an extremely high rating by the rowing community. If competition is at hand and time comparison are valued, -this machine should be the number one choice. Any of the machine's detractions are far outweighed by its almost perfect design. The machine's construction is elegant and a perfect example of form following function. More importantly, they can be unmercifully pounded on without any need for concern. The Concept2 has been the top choice for universities, gyms and rehabilitation clinics for as long as can be remembered. It works, works, works and breakdowns are rare. The Concept2 has gained a reputation as being "the 24/7 workhorse" for high volume gyms and for this reason alone, they have gained unwavering confidence.

With that said, there are slight problems. The pull rope, which is actually a chain, lacks the silence and longevity seen in synthetic ropes used by other manufacturers. These chains, while tough, do in fact need repair from time to time. As far a the noise goes, the fan, along with that of the chain, does generate a significant amount of sound. The new model D has addressed this NOISE issue with an enhanced sound dampening design. However, the Concept2 model D is still loud enough to bother some people. If noise considerations are on the top of your list, this machine may not be for you. However, there is another side to this argument which has validity. Some people actually like the built-in noise of these machines and personally speaking, I'm one of them. They definitely have a little snarl to them. Sometimes a little noise is a good thing! And here is a little hint; after you get used to the machine's sound, the noise can actually be used for pacing. There is a very noticeable difference in the cadence between slow, medium and fast rowing. The noise also tends to add a little excitement and vibrato to the experience. Many people want and love this!

The current Concept2 model D indoor rower is a little under 12 feet long and comes in at a slim 24 inches wide. Its maximum weight limit is a staggering 500 pounds with the regular seat. They even offer an online log book to keep track of your progress. Again, the concept2 model D is 900 dollars plus shipping.

It would seem the boys at Concept2 were not completely satisfied with the Model D and with such gnawing, the Model E was brought forth. In actuality, the model E is really not a different model than its predecessor; it's a high-seat model geared toward those having difficultly getting in-and-out of the lower seat version. Additionally, extra enhancements such as double powder coating, a nickel-plated chain and fully enclosed housing were added-in for good measure. Without question, the Model E has been geared towards high use facilities and rehab clinics. The Model E, while not specifically designed for home use, is available for anyone desiring a high-seat model. For all others, the Model D will more than suffice. At the time of this writing, the Model E is $1,260 (plus shipping). Both of the Concept2 models offer extended rails for exceedingly tall people. More information on the Concept2 can be found at:

http://www.concept2.com

Water Rower (Water-Based Model)

Our second indoor rower is the WaterRower. This machine is quite different from the Concept2 models. The WaterRower, as its name implies, offers the unique feature of water-based resistance via a water tank, submerged fan and a sprag clutch. This rowing machine has been long heralded as the most realistic rowing simulator on the market. Due to the engineering and water-based resistance, the motion feels silky smooth and as is often commented, very realistic. The net effect is a perfectly smooth motion which has the feeling of being properly balanced throughout the distance of the stroke. This gives what many consider to be the perfect distribution of upper to lower body division of work. Other machines seem to be close, but are slightly off in this area. The sound of lightly swishing water is surprising pleasant and often thought of as more meditative than disruptive. The WaterRower has one nice feature in that it utilizes an ultra-strong synthetic rope. As might be expected, these new synthetic ropes are incredibly strong, silent and seemingly impervious to wear. Add in a well-engineered clutch system and you have what is the perhaps one of the best rowers on the market. Many people who own these machines are fanatical about them and will accept nothing else!

With the WaterRower, if more intensity is desired, you simply row faster and you get increased intensity. If a runner wants more intensity, he or she simply runs faster! This is endurance exercise, not weightlifting, -a point which the people at WaterRower.com drive home again and again. Some people have tried to increase the resistance of the machine by adding additional water (WaterRower discounts this) or by adding additional elements (Epson Salts) to the water. In all honesty, such approaches are counterproductive. The WaterRower has been designed to be self regulating in terms of variable rowing speeds and corresponding work output for any given pace. In other words, if you want a more intense workout, there is not need to manually change any resistance settings from when rowing (previously) at slower speeds. It can be loosely thought of as automatic self regulation. As an interesting to note, not all large rowers enjoy increased resistance and many prefer the crisp feel of regular resistance coupled with faster rowing speeds. This is the way nature intended it and a hint for many newcomers. That being said, it's your machine and if "tweaking" is your desire, then feel free.

The brilliant design of this machine does not stop with the water resistance and well engineered clutch mechanism. The WaterRower is unique simply because it is made almost entirely of wood. People who have never seen the WaterRower are often shocked when first viewing its all wood frame. After all, how many mechanical items are made from wood nowadays. These wood based models add an element of grace and beauty which has yet to be duplicated in any other machine. Place these machines on a wood floor and you have an ascetic combination which cannot be beat. Most people try to hide their exercise equipment, -and in most cases, such practices are more than justified. The WaterRower is so good looking, placement in a living room proves to be no detraction whatsoever! This is perhaps the only rowing machine in which the worlds of art and science have been perfectly interwoven.

Most would assume wood to be too weak. Nothing could be farther from the truth. These machines utilize a dual rail system which has obtained an incredible level of strength. For many years, these machines were actually stronger in terms of their maximum load capacity than other models fashioned from metal. Somewhat surprisingly, they were not only stronger than other machines, but were sometimes more than doubling their competitors maximum weight limits. More than doubling maximum weight limits and made of all this wood? You bet and cheers to WaterRower on a fantastic design! The maximum weight limit for the WaterRower is 2,200 pounds. This is an amazing upper weight limit to say the least. Very few rowing machines can claim such samsonian strength.

Unlike many other machines, the WaterRower boasts of having zero maintenance. Given enough time, most other machines will require some maintenance, but with the WaterRower, repairs should be non-existent. As a side note, the user will have to occasionally replace water purification tablets in an effort to keep bacterial growths from occurring in the tank. These tablets are cheap and can be supplied from WaterRower.com or any swimming pool supplier. Other than that, the foot straps should be the only other item in need of occasional replacement. Again, these are also inexpensive.

For many, the beauty of the wood is the only way to go. However, WaterRower recently broke from tradition and added a completely new stainless steel (solid) version to their line. Crowned the "S" model, this elegant and exceeding modern looking rower was designed by their Germany office. Leave it to the Germans, they love their steel. If you like strong, elegant and shinny metallic designs, this one is for you. Without question, this model remains the crown jewel of the collection.

Not long after the addition of the stainless steel model, yet another metal-based model came forward. Dubbed the M model and coming with a more bulky/tubular appearance, this machine would be the first in the WaterRower lineup to add a high or low seat version. These tubular models lack much of the company's trademark ascetics and are solely designed for gym and rehabilitation conditions. While these M models are built like tanks, overcoming the poor ascetics is difficult after seeing the regular wood versions. That being said, the high seat models will come in handy for the elderly and those suffering from various injuries. Obviously, the people at WaterRower have been paying attention to consumers with special needs and these machines, while not as refined as their elegant siblings, serve a purpose.

The WaterRower checks in at just under seven feet in length and is obviously wider than most models due to its horizontally placed tank and dual rails. Overall, the water rower is not overly bulky and actually comes in a foot shorter in length than the Concept2. A choice of beautiful hardwoods is given and yes, some are more expensive than others. As a side note, selecting one hardwood over another will not significantly affect the strength of the machine, as these are primarily ascetic concerns. Let it be said again, the WaterRower's maximum weight limit is a staggering 2,200 pounds! Unbelievable as it sounds, they really are that strong! As an added bonus, city dwellers, along with all others dealing with cramped conditions, will enjoy the vertical stand-up ability of the WaterRower; no doubt, an appreciated feature for those in need. At the time of this writing, the cost of the WaterRower baseline model comes in at a tad over the 1,000 dollar mark, making it roughly comparable to the pricing on the Concept2 Model D. However, some models made from specialty woods, or metal, do come with an elevated price tag. At the extreme end, the "S" model comes in at 2,500 dollars. Although lofty, the price is more than justified; it's a thoroughbred worth every penny. Prices were calculated with the monitor included and you will want the monitor, so pay for it up front! After all, purism only goes so far! Everyone wants to know the metrics! Information provided by the monitors is desirable, even for those unconcerned with rankings and competition.

As with the Concept2, this rowing machine receives an outstanding rating. These machines, regardless of material, rank better than the Concept2 in the noise range. However, if you plan to race in large competitions such as BIRC or CRASH-B, this is may not be your machine. These machines do not have anything comparable to a damper. However, many individuals could care less about competitive rowing and in some cases, a repulsion is to be had for it. For them, it's all about the enjoyment of rowing and these purists tend to stick with the WaterRower. As mentioned before, the WaterRower will give you more noise reduction, more styling, more strength and with some models, a price tag in the "more" range. The machines from WaterRower are amazingly functional, exceedingly elegant, creatively designed and have managed to obtain a level of toughness rarely seen with such fine cultivation. In a nutshell, if Q were to design a rowing machine for Mr. Bond, this would be it. WaterRower models do offer extended rails for exceedingly tall people. Information on the WaterRower can be found at: http://www.waterrower.com

Where, What, and How to Buy

Concept2, along with WaterRower machines, can be purchased straight from the manufacturer. Taking this route is highly recommended whenever possible. Most retail outlets jack up the price far too high to justify any convenience. Some (not all) retailers offer delivery condition guarantees, free installation and will even go the extra mile with demonstrations. Could this expense be viewed as an exorbitant tax for absolutely nothing at all? In general, it only takes three minutes to show proper rowing form and free instructional videos litter the web. On the flip side, if local retailers are not too overpriced, such an option may be considered, but be sure to do some comparison shopping via company websites.

With two of the more easily identified models being reviewed, potential buyers should have gotten a pretty good idea of what to look for in a rower. The two reviewed machines are of the utmost quality and construction, however, buying from other manufacturers still remains an option. If going this route, please stay away from sub-par "department store" style models. In other words, the cheap-o models seen in some athletic stores. They are to be avoided at all costs. These weaker, or "toned down models," may be easier on the wallet, but no real savings are to be had in the long run. When it comes to rowing machines, consumers get what they pay for! It's better to save up and get a more durable model than to save a couple hundred bucks and have it break down. Not to mention, some (not all) of these discount rowers have poor mechanical designs, resulting in poor seat movement and non-uniform or jerky resistance. And one last thing, don't buy ugly rowing machines. The average price of a rowing machine comes in at 1,000 dollars; considering the price tag, models should at least be ascetically pleasing. Both the Concept2 and Water-Rower have good looks, but this is not true of all models, from all companies. Ugly and clunky looking machines made from gritty plastic should receive no attention whatsoever. A decent amount of cash is being spent and the machine's "looks" should be reflective of this simple fact. A "finished" appearance should more than dominate.

Buying a used machine is certainly a good money saving option, but make certain to test the machine for proper functioning. Finding a machine with NO damage is the goal. Be sure to verify the make, model and ask the owner as to why he or she is selling it. In general, weightlifting equipment, exercise bikes, elliptical machines, along with other fitness machines, are very easy to find. However, used rowing machines are extremely rare commodities and trying to find one is oftentimes easier said than done. Just to be sure, deal only with trusted sellers. And please, stay away from people selling long used equipment at prices slightly under the machine's original value. If it's used, a risk is being taken and buyers should demand pricing at half the original value or better yet, one-third. Yes, demand this pricing even if it appears to be in perfect condition and was only used twice! Used means "USED," so don't accept anything other than a great deal.

Chapter 7

Heart Rate Monitors

It's hard to look around in today's advanced society and not be keenly aware of sheer number of amazing inventions. Unfortunately, clever as each apparatus, black box and micro-chip filled gizmo may be, most have done little to lighten our load and added together, they are now doing more to overburdened us. Running water and toilets aside, we would be well advised to junk most of these modern advances. However, some of todays "extras" are providing great value and giving much in the way of safety and enhanced understanding. This is unquestionably true of heart rate monitors and yes, in our exercise deprived society, they should be placed right up there with running water and toilets. Let's take some time to go over the all-wonderful, all-telling heart rate monitors; one of histories least talked about, but greatest inventions.

A lot can be done with these gadgets that would not be suspec-
ted. With a heart rate monitor, participants can actually stop paying
attention to all the other information on the rowing machine monitor.
For example, participants can now do a workout for 25 minutes at a
sustained heart rate of 145 beats per minute. How far did they go?
-Well, who cares! How fast did they go? -Well, who cares! Sounds
simple and it is! Make no mistake here, the rowing machine's built-in
monitor provides a bounty of useful information; they generally have
various workouts, countdowns, timers, PC interfaces, along with ever
other imaginable way to plot progress. These "metrics" have been
demanded by the rowing community. However, some athletes (especially beginners) just want it simple and that's fine. With a heart rate
monitor being used at the most simplistic level, all that needs to be
given attention is the heart rate and time. That's it, -all of the guess-
work has been taken out of the equation. Immediate feedback is giv-
en and increasing or decreasing effort is all that is needed for staying
within a given heart rate range. Although simplistic, this "heart rate +
time" method for exercising is much beloved and traditionally
favored by people beginning weight loss programs. Not to mention,
doctors absolutely love this method; the danger of hyper-elevated
heart rates is easily avoided and the lack of variables keeps it simple
for both parties. When young and in good health, such concerns are
generally unwarranted, but when optimal circumstances are lacking,
correct measurement is paramount for both you and the doctor.

For well conditioned athletes beginning a new regimen, the heart rate monitors can be used as a protective mechanism while improving health. Even for those somewhat fit, entering high heart rate zones should not be attempted in the early going. And let this point be very clear! **Under no circumstances should a newbie be jumping into the heart rate zones designed for the ultra-fit.** A certain level of health, along with enhanced physical development, should be obtained before doing so and here is where using heart rate monitors for time-stepped graduations comes in handy. Please, allow for some adaptation to occur, -then and only then, can the "Rocky Balboa" dreams of being the champ can be given play. For anyone beginning an exercise routine, visiting the doctor is a good idea. By way of stress test, along with other testing procedures, a great deal of certainty can be gained, -one way or the other! Do NOT discount the importance of doctors in this realm. This is especially true if exercise has not been undertaken for some time and for anyone getting up there in years. And no, getting up there in years does not mean over 70 years old; it means over 25 years old. Doctors can be used for finding the initial starting points and the heart rate monitors can be used for staying in those zones and making safe time-stepped graduations.

Heart rate monitors derive great benefit from their Mickey Mouse level of complexity. No put down is being made here! Easy metrics allow for a participants to stay within target zones and more importantly, to avoid the more demanding regions. Again, this is particularly important for people who are beginning an exercise program and especially for those who are overweight. Obese people especially, along with the out-of-shape among us, can get their heart rate going into the red-line zone with nothing more than moderate effort and this red-line potential is hastened during hot/humid weather. And there is no need to mention the importance of these heart rate monitors for people who have heart disease, along with other risk factors; a self evident factor, as far as "red-line" prevention is concerned!

Recommendations for specific heart rate levels, or for that matter, any given ranges, will not be made. Again, self-analysis and medical testing remain paramount for figuring the numbers. Everyone has different fitness levels, recuperative abilities and far too many other health factors to recommend specific ranges or goals. For now, and throughout the beginning stages, use heart rate monitors for keeping a steady rate and avoiding more dangerous zones. Heart rate monitors are great for keeping on track and out of trouble.

Chapter 8

Your First Row

Before the preliminary workouts are attempted, the topic of conditioning needs to be covered. When beginning a rowing regimen, many participants will have already acquired a fantastic level of conditioning. However, many more will be appallingly out-of-shape and this is unfortunately true of the more youthful segments of our population. Living in developed nations is very different now, from what it was 40 years ago. Advice and warnings which would at one time have only applied to those over 45 years of age are now applicable to youngsters. Our societal obsession with sedentary activities has paved the way for ill-health and has inundated itself to such a degree, as to effortless work its way down to the youngest and most weight tolerant individuals among us. Most youngsters of the past could be heard saying, "I cannot gain weight, -no matter how much I eat." We aren't hearing those sort of statements being made anymore. For most in this modern age, adoption of rowing routine is done to get in shape, -and not for a desire to stay in shape. There are a few exceptions to this rule, but these exceptions are becoming more and more rare.

After watching a gazillion "get-fit" TV shows, with boot camp style instructors trying like maniacs to get flabby people into rock hard condition, -a little more than an eyebrow has to be raised. These supposedly knowledgeable instructors, passing themselves off as experts, are clueless. I have almost passed out watching them make severely obese people start running. Running when obese should never be done! Joint destruction will occur in no time flat. Being severely overweight is bad enough for your joints as it is, but the impact from running is a death sentence for them. Additionally, watching these so-called trainers place obese people on skinny seated exercise bikes has been almost nauseating to watch. Imagine how much pressure is being placed on their perineums. Take one of these instructors and place 90+ pounds worth of sandbags on their backs and see how well he or she feels on a skinny bike seat! Most of these instructors have no idea what is like to be out of shape and remain clueless to the safe training procedures for the obese. Severely overweight people should never engage vertical weight bearing exercises and there are no exceptions to this rule. Surprisingly, very tall people, due to heavier bodies, along with leverage issues, have the same problem. This "tall dilemma" presents itself even for those who are lean and in good condition. Go on any team airplane after a NBA game and look at how many of these boys have ice bags on their swollen knees. Why is this occurring and what exactly is the condition of such players? Are they cardio trained? -Yes. Are they specimens of perfect physical health? -Yes. Do these players have low body fat levels? -Yes Do these athletes have low body weights and leverage advantages? -NO. They have extremely heavy bodies and increased joint stress due to leverage issues corresponding to longer limbs. Being extremely tall (even when lean) can actually be worse than being short and moderately overweight. For individuals who are are heavy for whatever reason, certain exercises have to be permanently avoided. End of story.

The second offense by questionable instructors, deals not with the exercise type, but a foolish demand for out-of-shape (heavy or not) participants to be given such intense workouts. This entertaining notion of taking out-of-shape slobs and putting them through a G. I Joe style ringer, provides for nothing more than foolish entertainment; that is, entertainment at their expense. Would anybody, with any level of common sense, take a old car, with tons of damage and enter it in the Daytona 500. Of course not, -the car would have to be slowly worked on, tested, balanced and improved to the point of being race worthy. The human body is absolutely no different and those undergoing such demands, without proper conditioning and development, have nothing more to look forward to than becoming overly sore, burned-out and in some cases, injured. Adding jet fuel to the fire, trainers often propel these poorly conditioned souls into cross-training regimens. Strike three! They are oftentimes doing dangerous exercises, being overworked to the nth degree and then drained of valuable healing reserves. And if that was not enough, they are further overtaxed by unfamiliar exercises. When considering the latter, proponents of cross-training will proudly speak of maximum muscle fiber recruitment resulting from a lack of exercise adaptation and the corresponding increases in caloric expenditure. Again, no errors have be made with regard to theoretical correctness of cross-training, but the outcomes often look nothing like what is on paper. Sustained caloric burning, for months and years, is more feasible when approached from a single exercise for which proper conditioning has occurred. This way, the participants can go the distance, without injury, high levels of pain, or any need for excessive recuperation time. Otherwise, BURNOUT will act as a brick wall. This adaptation takes weeks! Actually, it takes months or even years for "this" true adaptation to take hold. This cross-training theory is sick lie which pays no mind to proper conditioning, adaptive response, physiology or psychology. It is nothing more than a baby bird that wanted to fly, but lacked the muscular and aerobic conditioning to do so. As can easily be seen, strike four, five and six, are not far behind.

For those out of shape, or carrying a few extra pounds, indoor rowing serves as deservedly biased option for the restructuring of a body so resistant to the unreasonable expectations of traditional training. No Running, No biking, No sit-ups, No jumping rope, No tennis, No Golf, No soccer, No skating, No basketball, and NO...NO...NO..., not anything else. It's now time to experience a little taste of perfection in exercise. Get on the machine and strap your feet in. Your first row will only be for seven minutes. People are the funniest things; it is not uncommon for first time rowers to get on a machine and start clamoring about the ease; five minutes later, they are out of gas and dying! Rowing machines are exceedingly deceptive for newcomers! People tend to compare them to the effort of running and they just don't work that way. Unlike running, your upper body takes on some of the load, along with the machine bearing much of the weight and as a result, it seems exceedingly easy at first.

I am assuming you now have your own rowing machine or at least have access to one. There are only two major rules for rowing. Folks, it does not get any easier than this. Rowing is simple and very natural, -please remember this!

1. Rule number one: Don't "death grip" the handle! Keep a nice relaxed overhand grip on the handle. The chain/hook grip, with the fingers curled in a "U" shape, is strongest possible grip for a human. There is no need to death grip the handle. So relax the hands.

2. Rule number two: Don't engage the arms until the end of the movement.

Rule number two is the single biggest mistake rookies make and it's a critical one. Keep your arms straight for the first part of the movement and only start bending them at the end of the drive. This way, the legs do the majority of the work and the upper body finishes the movement. For those not following this advice, a rude awakening will come about, by way of the arms quickly burning out. Keep the arms straight and only initiate the pull once the legs have just (not 100%) about fully extended. Easy enough! Other mistakes do happen, but they are incredibly rare due to rowing being such a natural movement.

Yup, that's it, -and how nice is that? Only two things to remember. Rowing is simple! There is one other matter which should to be given attention during the early stages. When rowing is first undertaken, the legs will typically want to bow out after some time; this will be easily understood about three minutes into your first row. Don't worry about "leg bowing" when it happens, -just allow it to occur. As time goes on, corrections can be made through conditioning. After all, these are not exactly muscles which get used every day!

Phase 1

A good rule of thumb is to have beginners row seven minutes a day for the first 2 weeks. During this time, refrain from sprinting or anything else which might be considered fast pacing. The idea is to get the muscles accustomed to the movement and nothing more. You have the rest of your life to row, -there is no hurry! As an alternative for those with a good amount of youth induced vigor, or for those already in good shape, ten minutes a day can be done. Don't worry, the body's sensory feedback system is exceedingly chatty and a little state of the union address will be issued after the first couple of rows. Is soreness setting in? Is that oh-so common "drained" feeling taking hold? Is rowing getting harder during subsequent sessions or is it creating an energized state? These are all factors in need of personal analysis and not something to be guided by external means; everyone is different in this regard. If finding yourself somewhat sore or lacking good recovery, this may not be a bad thing. Such factors may be a signal of more initial recovery time being needed, or perhaps a simple indication of being extremely out of shape. The rational for addressing "soreness" and "fatigue" may seem strange when such a limited amount of exercise is being undertaken. The rowing movement, while graceful and very natural, utilizes muscles in a far different manner than everyday activities. The legs are bending deeply (even farther than deep knee squats) and functionally utilizing muscles which are almost never used in everyday exercise. The same goes for the lower back. As a result, some people tend to get very sore in the beginning. Others will feel nothing at all.

Phase 2

After this two-week introduction period, advancement to a four-week cycle of 15 minutes per day can be done. Again, keep the pace nice and slow! No effort is being made to oust champion rowers from their top spots. Time is being taken to build endurance in the muscles corresponding to the rowing movement. This takes time, -so don't rush things. Engaging in high intensity rowing would be the worst possible thing for any beginner to consider at this point. Don't even think about it! Doing so would most certainly result in severe soreness and even for those not becoming overly sore, a feeling of depletion will eventually take hold. Under such circumstances, the ability to maintain day-to-day rowing becomes questionable and in the end, multiple days are typically skipped, -with rowing easily becoming a forgotten activity. People want to keep rowing, but lose their drive due to burnout. Their bodies were not ready for the volume or intensity and the penalty for overtaxing an untrained system becomes more than apparent. General malaise, decreased drive and that "tapped-out" feeling are all too common reminders of what it's like to be in such a compromised state. Remember, time is being taken not only for muscular conditioning, but also for the heart, lungs and circulatory system to develop. Not to mention, other not so obvious adaptations are taking place with regard red blood cell adaptation, motor pathway development and the like. Complete restructuring from the most minuscule biochemical level, to the gross musculature is taking place. So relax, -keep it nice n' slow with short rows in the beginning and obey the speed limit. This early overexertion problem is actually more dangerous for fit individuals than it is for unfit ones. Generally speaking, an unfit person will be kept from overexertion simply because of an inability to go into overdrive during the initial stages. They just get fatigued too easily and will typically self-moderate for reasons of fatigue and pain management. As for the in-shape crowd, they can generally go harder in the beginning, with less soreness and no fatigue. This is often deceptive because better conditioned athletes have systems which can endure more abuse in the early rounds, but have not yet truly adapted to the exercise. Consequently, they can often push themselves into hyper-elevated realms of fatigue and not really feel it. For them, full intensity is maintained until a brick wall is struck. It takes longer, but the effect is often worse in terms of quitting the exercise. Essentially, they can drive themselves into the ground much harder and once they realize the problem, they are in too deep to get out. Again, please head the warning! The regularity of this mistake being made is astonishing. After this four-week cycle, things should be going well.

Phase 3

We now move onto our third phase of conditioning. On this rung of the ladder, 20 minutes a day, at a pace between low and moderate will be done. No insult will be made and pacing can be self judged. Again, stay away from anything near a snail's pace and do not consider anything faster than the low end of moderate. Please continue this cycle for two months.

Congratulations, actual rowing is taking place and some of the benefits should already be starting to show. At this point, adaptation is still occurring, which is why this phase is drawn out for two months. As with the introductory period, the importance of this two-month training period cannot be stressed enough and any thoughts of side-stepping it should be immediately discarded. Slight changes in body composition should be more than apparent at the end of this two-month stage and in some cases, such changes will be dramatic. Staying with this phase can be done a long as desired, but remember to keep with it for a minimum of two months. Nice and easy, nothing fast!

Chapter 9

Main Rowing Regimens

After completing the first three phases, adoption of one of more serious rowing regimens may be undertaken. The first is a favorite of the masses and much admired for its simplicity. Be forewarned, the plainness of this routine should in no way allow for it to be viewed as inferior; it has led to more goal achievement and received more adulation than any other. It's maintainable, enjoyable and highly effective! The second routine, designed with the ultra-fit in mind and consisting of multiple sprints with the specific intention of massively decreasing fat stores, serves as the crème de la crème of fitness routines. While not designed for the masses, this option takes a stab at perfection. Those desiring a high retention of muscle mass, while maintaining an unbelievable level of leanness, -have finally found their answer; the results are too good to be true and the required effort, -far too brutal to be fair. The third is simply an alternative to the second, -minus the undulating nature of the sprints and the ultra-high intensity; undoubtedly a good option for those wanting a more vigorous workout, but without such extremes. The forth and final choice consists of high intensity sprints which are short in number, short in rest period duration, but amazingly fruitful when it comes to massive bi-directional increases in both strength and endurance. This workout can be used in and of itself with regard to rowing, but is better suited for conditioning athletes outside of rowing; the number of sports which could benefit from such training goes on-and-on. There is one last exercise regimen which solely focuses on competition and do to the complexity of subject matter, an entire chapter (12) has been dedicated to it in an effort to fully cover the topic. It will serve as a much needed guide for anyone seriously considering competition and wanting to win.

Option 1: The 20 Minute Routine

(first 6 months, mandatory for all)

This is as simple as is it gets and nothing more than 20 minutes at moderate pacing is expected. Nothing flashy is going on here and it's a great workout. This workout is really no different than the aforementioned phase three, -with the only exception being the intensity. In this case, moderate intensity is demanded and low intensity is forbidden. Don't worry, with 20 minutes, plenty of time will be had for calorie burning. Take note, -due to the the increased intensity, the effortless nature of the previous workouts will soon give way to sweat n' tears. With rowing working to split the workload, less perceived work output is generally observed with the lighter workouts, but these workouts will put an end to that. In other words, these can really be felt. It is hard, but not too hard. A good rule of thumb is to do this regimen for four to five days per week and add some other form of activity on the weekends. However, some people will want to keep rowing almost every day. For anybody falling into this category, weekends can be used for shorter sprinting races. Ultimately, it's a matter of personal preference and what any given person can handle. Remember though, the crux of this workout is mid-range, moderate rowing. Make sure the word "moderate" means moderate and NOT sprinting. Those foolish enough to attempt 20 minute long workouts at sprinting pace will be left saying, "I really shouldn't have done that." And that statement will unfortunately be uttered for the next few days! Additionally, "moderate" does not mean putting as much effort forward as in, uh, let's say, casual jogging or casual swimming; it's more akin to fast running, but not sprinting. Fast running is NOT how most people would define moderate, but that's our definition. This 20 minute regimen should be done for at least six months before any other workouts are considered. That being said, -participants could actually stop here and row this way for the rest of their lives and be just fine.

Many will follow this path and the best long term answer is often found in this highly challenging, but simplistically designed regimen. Keep in mind, moving on is not demanded and further advancement may not be the best answer. For those feeling the call of wild and wanting to take a step into more elite testing grounds, please read on.

2: HIIT (High Intensity Interval Training)

Here is where things start to change and a little more science gets added into the mix. This workout is for athletes who have reached a high level of cardiovascular fitness and have bodies properly adapted for intense rowing. This program is **VERY** difficult and requires a ramping-up period.

For years, effective fat burning was only considered possible by way of way long endurance-based exercises, typically spanning 30+ minutes. After about 25-30 minutes, glycogen levels drop to almost nil and the body then starts burning fat as the primary fuel; it is this post 30 minute period when all the splendid re-sculpturing takes place. This unquestioned dogma, fittingly described as the "fat burning zone," has been the gold standard for weight loss types and other self described fitness gurus for decades. Oh yes, it does in fact establish leanness, but at what cost? The cost is little to no preservation of muscle mass, injuries galore and once undamaged, spry body systems, now being left worn and tattered. Not exactly enticing, now is it?

In recent years, many have rightfully questioned the "long distance" logic. Such inquiries may have resulted from observing sprinters' low body fat levels. It only took a few decades of watching them on television, with ripped abs and muscles galore, -to finally wise up and started asking some questions. It may also have been due to people looking for an alternative to the injury ridden endurance based workouts. Perhaps it was just a desire to have a short, time saving workouts, that preserved muscle mass. The fact of these sprinters having such low body fat levels, such short workouts, and still yet, abundant muscle to boot, was interesting, if not vexing. During the early going, some people had hinted at these facts, but nobody would ever go against the almighty "fat burning zone" training system without adequate proof. Even today, most experts still recommend doing a minimum of 30+ minutes of cardio a couple times a week. What that really means is doing 45-60 minutes of cardio each and every day. After all, if the body doesn't burn fat until roughly 30 minutes into the workout, then more and more time must be put in after the first 30 minutes. With the first 30 minutes serving as little more than a primer for fat burning, -a huge waste of time is occur- ring!

New studies have shown this old methodology to be less than optimal. Shorter workouts with segmented periods of sprinting, work far better at decreasing fat stores than older methodologies concerning "fat burning zone" style (45-60 minutes), straight low intensity endur- ance workouts. Not only this, but the new high intensity training res- ults in a high degree of muscle mass being retained. Additionally, it may actually stimulate hormone production just as much as heavy weightlifting and this little bonus is worth more than its weight in gold. The formal name of this amazing program is High Intensity In- terval Training, or HIIT for short. For this discovery, we all owe a debt of gratitude to a man by the name of Dr. Tremblay. His work has raised many eyebrows in the scientific community, at least for those who were willing to listen.

In Dr. Tremblay's research, subjects engaging in HIIT lost over three times as much body fat compared to those doing longer duration cardio workouts. [1] Over three times, -this is truly an amazing. And considering the youthfulness of the subjects (college students), the results were startling. After all, the subjects being studied didn't exactly have massive amounts of fat to shed. These were healthy, in--shape college kids and not the sedentary, plumped-up cubicle workers of today's mega-corps. With this understanding, a threefold increase in fat loss can be considered dramatic when considering the situational factors! As a somewhat surprising finding, the comparison group (engaging in longer duration exercises) was shown to have greater total energy outputs over the HIIT group. Such findings are very illogical considering the results. Anyone having greater energy output should in fact have a higher caloric expenditure and as logic would follow, greater fat burning. Yeah, that would certainly make sense, but not in this case. The "three times" higher fat loss in the HIIT group is theorized by some to be due to more total carbs being burned in these workouts. Such reasoning may be a little bit lean for explaining totality of fat burning seen during the HIIT routine. Further explanations, based on complex biochemical findings, point to large metabolic increases occurring throughout the day, along with other effects, such as strong appetite suppression. Truth be told, the fat-lady has not exactly sung when it comes to full accounting for the superiority of the HIIT routine. However, the auxiliary explanations are well grounded and provide for a more balanced view of what more of today's scientists are leaning towards in terms of explanation. It can be rightfully stated that these workouts (HIIT) burn an amazing amount of fuel when being done and really stoke the metabolic engine long afterward. Any other uncertainties are of little consequence, -and with the results being understood, the scientists can be left to button-up the remaining loose-ends in their own good time.

Despite the biochemical complexity of high intensity interval training, the routine itself is actually very simple to understand. For HIIT, a short 15 minute workout is all it takes and unlike many standard workouts, HIIT adds-in the colorful twist of repeated sprints. Participants begin by sprinting for 30 seconds, then resting for 30 seconds, -and continuation of "this" cycle is done for 15 minutes. As a side note on the sprinting time, -humans cannot really sprint at full capacity for more than 30 seconds. If sprints were to be carried out any longer, well..., that's not really sprinting. As for the 30 second rest cycles, just enough time is given for heart rate deceleration and a quick catching-of-the-breath before the next sprinting cycle takes place. During the rest cycles, keep rowing, but at a very slow pace. Think of the rest cycles as super slow jogging. In other words, keep moving, but not much faster than a snail's pace.

As always, taking it slow is the key. Most of us have not sprinted since childhood and even then, it may not have been a common activity. Kids run a great deal, but rarely sprint at full speed. To eventually be able to complete the full 15 minutes with alternating sprints and rests, a progressive approach, based on a 15-week ramp-up schedule should be undertaken. During the first week, only one of 30 second sprints will be done for the entire 15 minute program. For the remaining 14 minutes and 30 seconds, -rowing at the higher end of the moderate scale will be done. During week two, two sprints during the 15 minute program will be done. During week three, -three sprints will be done. That's it! Just keep working up the ladder by adding one more sprinting cycle per week. Just remember to give yourself a 30 second rest period in between sprints. Progression can be self-paced and allowances can be made for additional rest time if needed. So, what exactly constitutes true sprinting? Sprinting, by technical definition, is 90-95% of the participant's VO2 Max. Total V02 Max (100%) is useful to rowers, but on-the-fly measurements (variable percentages of V02 Max) are all but impossible without in-mouth hoses, laboratory equipment and computers. In this case, dropping the numbers is recommended. Stick with a close, real-world approximation. Everybody knows what sprinting is, -we all did it at as children. Yes, you're permitted to wing it! Sprints should be done at full gut-busting intensity; after each 30 seconds sprint, the leg muscles should feel as though they are burning masses of gelatin and the lungs, -struggling to keep up. This is a good descriptive of what 90-95% feels like and in all honesty, exactly what should be expected from normal sprinting. Any greater metrical accuracy can be left to the white-coated geeks occupying the sports labs. More on VO2 Max will be given in the next chapter, but for now, let's continue with the ins-and-outs of the HIIT routine.

With HIIT, the importance of the rest periods in bringing the heart rate down, is often overlooked. For those struggling, incrementing the rest period cycles for a few extra seconds can be done as needed. Participants can define a "few" rather liberally, but keep in mind, the idea is to eventually back it down to the 30 second standard. It's also of equal importance not to let your heart rate go too high! As would be guessed, heart rate monitors come in very handy when engaging in HIIT and under no circumstances should they be excluded for this particular exercise program. People are highly variable when it comes to heart rate normalization times, along with what it takes to bring the heart up to excessive speeds. That's it for instruction and putting forth the needed effort is all that is left.

As a side note, participants will clearly not be able to do all of the sprints at the same level of intensity. This is certainly normal and should be expected. During the latter sprints, everything is going to start burning and the pain will feel as though it's increasing exponentially. It is these last couple of sprints, as the body's resources start to dwindle, that will prove to be excruciatingly difficult. Anyone in good enough shape can get through the first couple, but it's the last half which will separate the men from the boys.

These workouts are not for the weary and your body must have the physical capacity to do them safely. Folks, what can be expected from these workouts is nothing less than amazing! For starters, how about a chiseled mid section and by chiseled, I mean ripped to the bone. Some just might consider such claims to be a bit of a joke. Is there little bit of fibbing going on here? Absolutely not, -no deception of any kind is being put forth and these workouts are as amazing as they sound. As mentioned before, HIIT is extremely brutal and takes some preconditioning, so please be patient. In the end, the results are worth all the pain and agony. Those who have partaken in these workouts for some time, report being in a ripped condition, which they, nor anyone else would have ever thought possible. And that is the plain and simple reality of what these workouts can achieve! Ripped to the bone and carrying a good amount of muscle, what an exquisite combination! Always remember, a three times increase in body fat burning over conventional longer duration endurance training is occurring. For most people, Dr. Tremblay is not a household name, but he has unearthed what is perhaps the most important scientific study on enhanced fat burning to ever be published!

Well, that's it for the HIIT, or is it? Just as the dust was about settle and people started warming up the the realities of HIIT, Dr. Tremblay would release another study which would further boost the already mushrooming popularity of HIIT. In 1994, a study from Canada's Laval University recorded a NINE times increase in subcutaneous fat burning (HIIT) compared to that of longer duration endurance exercise. Nine times, ARE YOU CRAZY! What happened to three? Personally speaking, these results need to be replicated and verified before references are made, but if the findings are accurate, or at least close, this will mark the final triumph for HIIT.

Alternative Workout to HIIT, Welcome to the 8-5-3

For many, enduring 15 minutes of high intensity interval training is just far too excruciating. After all, it is called HIGH INTENSITY for a reason! Many people are in good enough shape to take on an enhanced workout, but may lack the capacity for the elite HIIT. Questions of capacity aside, some rowers dislike HIIT for a very interesting reason. The rapidly undulating nature of the HIIT routine produces a certain jaggedness, which hasn't exactly been embraced by those enjoying the rhythmical, almost clock-like nature of rowing. There is a certain logic to this argument which cannot be discredited. For many, rowing is about keeping a fairly steady pace and enjoying the natural rhythm of the machine; this is true, regardless of speed. With that said, a secondary advanced program is offered, which turns up the heat, but works to lessen the demanding nature and sharp edges of HIIT.

With 16 minutes of total workout time, it's roughly the same duration as HIIT. The extra minute (at the end) accounts for no substantial effort and simply allows for more gradual heart rate deceleration. The first eight minutes are a warm up. And "warm up," in this case, is understood to be gentle rowing, but not so gentle as to be crawling. This is not an eight minute rest period! For the next five minutes, participants are to row at 75% of their maximum heart rate. Keep it steady at 75% all the way through for five minutes. Finally, a three minute cool down period is added at the end to give a nice, gentle, slopped reduction in heart rate. This workout keeps the intensity up but stays away from the whole "race and slow down" situation found in HIIT.

By now, the following should be echoing in your brain: "Take it slow." It may have been a while since you exercised at 75% (Max HR) for five straight minutes. This workout may be a little harder than expected. I've never liked surprises and it's doubtful that you're any different. To avoid any problems, only add one minute at 75% for each week. For example, the first workout during week one would look as follows:

> 8 minute warm up
>
> 1 minute at 75%
>
> 7 minute cool down

For a total of 16 minutes

Week two would be

> 8 minute warm up
>
> 2 minutes at 75%
>
> 6 minute cool down

And so on, and so on............

It is all very simple, -just continue along each week and add one additional minute to the middle period and subtract one from the last cool down period. By the end of five weeks, the following will be done:

> 8 minute warm up
>
> 5 minutes at 75%
>
> 3 minute cool down

For those wondering, the warm up and cool down sessions are roughly the same, but expect to be doing the cool down period at a slightly decreased level of intensity and this is especially true for the very last minute; the idea is to tapper down to almost nothing at the end. Please don't take this workout as an easier option for getting out of HIIT. This workout is DIFFICULT and works wonderfully for those desiring more intense training, -but not the nth degree radicalism seen in HIIT. For those in the extremely fit category, upping the percentage past 80 will be advantages. Likewise, for those in lesser shape, the given percentage can be set below 75. In other words, this workout can be tailored to any given fitness level. The given percentage of 75% is little more than an arbitrary example. In the end, setting the percentage is a matter of personal choice, but the greater the intensity during the middle five minutes, the greater the fat burning! For those in search of more hardcore percentages being utilized by somewhat better conditioned athletes, -it's 83% to 86%. Ultra-elite athletes can push the percentages even further if desired.

Super Intense Tabata Sprints

The world of sports science appears to be full of wonderful discoveries. This is certainly true for advancements in human nutrition, but the same cannot be said for breakthroughs in human training systems. Since the inception of modern exercise (~1950-1970), there has been very little to report on. The boring synopsis of decades worth of sports research was as follows: "**LIFT WEIGHTS AND GET BIGGER, -RUN LONGER AND GET LEANER.**" Before the angry retorts storm in, clear acknowledgment is being given to the many discoveries and advancements over the last of couple of decades. However, the overwhelming majority of these discoveries were not appropriately situated to find themselves interwoven with the training regimens of the day, or even what would become the training systems of tomorrow. For decade after decade, the status quo locked-in with the simplified "bigger" or "thinner" mentality and any hope for elegant procedural changes were dismal. Little did anybody know, very blue skies were ahead and the late 1980s would kickoff a massive up-swing in training sophistication. This time period (1987-1997) would see a decade worth of highly unusual and significant advances, which added together, would mark a period of scientific sports advancement never yet seen; it was truly the decade of enlightenment. Information was spewing forth from private, public and academic sources at an incredibly accelerated rate, -to the point of making proper analysis difficult. It was almost as if the wheels of science gained critical momentum. With little surprise, this surge corresponded directly with the advent of modern computers becoming widely available, along with more hardy Internet development. This decade would see the denial of ultra-long endurance based exercises, the acceptance of shortened workouts (20 minutes at increased intensity), the advancement of HIIT and would finalize with the amazing discovery of Tabata sprints, which would serve as a beautiful bookend to a very fruitful and progressive decade.

The latter study, conducted by Dr. Izumi Tabata, Ph. D., of the Nation Institute of Health & Nutrition, utilized extremely hard (170% VO2 Max) 20 second sprints with exceedingly short 10 second rest periods. Only six to eight of these sprints were done per workout. The routine itself is obviously shorter than HIIT and added together, three minutes of total sprinting is all that's done per workout. What also differs is the intensity of the sprints. These sprints are to be done at a pace resulting in complete exhaustion by the end of 20 seconds. Plainly stated, "these sprints are done at an extreme level of intensity, with full-out, excruciating effort being demanded. Again, each sprint is to be attacked with maximum intensity and nothing else is expected! What should also be noted and is perhaps vastly more important, is the ten second rest periods. Such shortening is highly purposeful, if not sadistic and done in an attempt to place exceedingly heavy adaptive stress upon the aerobic system. Essentially, these participants, subjects, athletes, or whatever you want to call these poor downtrodden souls, -are about to find out what it is like to be gasping for oxygen and then forced to engage in another sprint, with each iteration thereafter becoming more grueling. The heavy hand of adaptation is clearly seen is this workout. The intensity is cruel, -almost to the point of being merciless. And yes, a developed, evolved and highly refined form of torture when done correctly. Tabata sprints are not for the timid or faint of heart.

The most interesting tidbit coming out of the Tabata study was the discovery of a "sweet spot" for maximization of both aerobic and anaerobic systems. Could it even be possible to find a regimen that maximally stressed both the anaerobic and aerobic systems simultaneously? The shocking answer seems to be yes! The highly intense 20 second sprints nail the anaerobic side of things, while the super short 10 second rest periods maximally stress the lungs. The result is an almost perfect 100% stress being placed on the anaerobic and aerobic systems simultaneously. If tweaking these numbers (sprint:rest time) a little, different levels of anaerobic vs. aerobic stress could be obtained.

You're probably wondering what specific increases were seen to support this notion of maximally stressed anaerobic and aerobic systems. This is the amusing part! First time viewers of these numbers are shocked and more often than not, pass them off as mere typos. Unbelievable as it may seem, no mistakes were made. In just 14 weeks, subjects on this protocol increased their VO2 max by 14%, while at the same time, anaerobic levels were reported to increase by a gigantic 28 percent.[2] By the way, 14% is an extremely high number for an increase in VO2 max! Given that these subjects were already in good shape, this number is undoubtedly huge. The 28 percent increase in anaerobic levels speaks for itself, -this is massive! It seems so obvious to maximally stress the aerobic system via short rest periods, while fully pressurizing the anaerobic side of things via all-out, short 20 second sprints. Seems simple in retrospect and everything does, -at least when viewed from this perspective. There is a lesson to be learned from this study. This program showed that less could actually be more. The secret to this less-is-more "result" seems to be rooted in the ultra-short rest periods. As an interesting side note, Dr. Tabata tested another program using two minute rest periods and with this program, strongly depreciated results were seen.

The workout itself consists of doing six to eight very hard sprints (20 seconds) with ten second rest periods between each. As with all the other regimens, an "ease-in" period is to be utilized before full intensity is applied. Unlike the previous "ramp-up" schedules, participants should initially do the entire workout (with all sprints) but at a low intensity level and only increase the intensity over the course of a few months. Use common sense and judge it for yourself.

As a side note, Tabata sprints do come at a price. Exhaustion from these workouts reaches a point whereby participants sometimes collapse off the rowing seat when finished. No exaggeration is being made, -the intensity level is enough to incapacitate. These workouts were developed for Olympic level competitors and even they had trouble with them. Tabata sprints are truly riding the lightning and with such razored intensity, certain problems are to be had. With the increased speed and intensity, both the risk of injury and the risk of having a cardiac event go up. Now granted, the risk of injury on a rowing machine remains low, but it could still happen. More important than injury is the increased risk of cardiac problems and alarmingly, these increases have also been noted in healthy subjects. Tabata based sprints, while being a little riskier, do in fact lead to a state of super-fitness. Super-fitness, while being very interesting in--and-of itself, seems to have little benefit on the general health of individuals. There are no great increases in the general health between fit vs. super fit humans. Being in good condition is just as good as super-fitness when it comes to general health. Furthermore, risk of disease and sickness are not decreased when advancing from VERY GOOD, to SUPER GOOD conditioning. The human body seems to have a thing for moderation.

So why include this workout routine? I honestly don't believe most people would even be able to do the Tabata sprints at full intensity. I also don't believe most people should do such workouts at the prescribed level of intensity. Folks, it's not the sprints that will punish you, -it's the short rest periods. Not to mention, Tabata sprints were solely designed for athletes in elite condition. However, there is a segment of our population which requires superb conditioning in the respective realms of both anaerobic and aerobic. It is this super-fit-ness which is needed for many hardcore competition scenarios and with the Tabata protocol, an unbeatable formula for victory is forged. Let's face it, -so much of competitive success comes down to how much gas is left in the tank at the end of a match. For those who have to reach the zenith in both directions, Tabata sprints provide a decis-ive advantage. I will say it again, "it's not for most people," but you can't say the results are anything less than amazing. There are many professional sports which could benefit from this training. Most op-ponents would rather crawl naked over broken glass than compete against a Tabata trained athlete. It's true!

Chapter 10

Understanding VO2 Max

The discussion of VO2 Max is well placed for after the workouts and comes in handy for some last minute cleanup work. VO2 Max, even when not being directly utilized, should at least be minimally understood by rowers. Unless having been in the position of "sports scientist," or that of a lab rat, -brushing shoulders with the VO2 Max may not have been a common occurrence. Most people describing themselves as athletically inclined will understand VO2 Max to be a measure of oxygen utilization, but failings with the finer details are not uncommon. This measuring stick, once reserved for only sports scientists and medical professionals, is now seeing increased uptake among everyday athletes. Most of the new adoption is due to VO2 max becoming unencumbered in terms of measurement ease. Yes, as unencumbered as heart rate measurement.

By definition, VO2 Max is the maximum amount of oxygen consumed at the greatest physical output. At some point during maximum exertion, the "body" as a whole, will no longer be able to take in more oxygen and this maximal numeric is known as VO2 Max. Oxygen, in this case, is measured in milliliters and finalized as the amount used in one minute per kilogram of body weight. Men generally have a slightly higher VO2 Max than women. Actually, men can have up to a 15-30% advantage in terms of VO2 Max and these differences are largely thought to be due to women having higher body fat percentages than their male counterparts. Regardless of any given starting point, VO2 Max can be improved by steady repetition of cardio training. VO2 Max asserts itself as one of the best single measurement tools for prognosticating competitive success. Trust me, it is no accident that Greg LeMond had such a high VO2 Max level (exceeding 90) and experienced massive success in competitive biking. Keep in mind, Mr. LeMond's high VO2 Max level may not have been the only reason for success, but it was a major one.

When accounting for any given VO2 Max score, dependencies, with relation to prominent factors, are that of the health/age of the lungs, heart, blood vessels and as would be assumed, the overall conditioning of the body. Additionally, the ability of the muscles to utilize oxygen and their corresponding recovery rates also play a role; in other words, its a two way street between the muscles and the systems that support them. In almost every case, VO2 Max can be substantially increased through endurance training. With that said, some people are obviously more gifted in this area than others. Most people could train ever day for the rest of their lives and never reach the VO2 Max score of Greg LeMond. As with almost everything else, genetics plays a strong role and VO2 Max is no exception. Even so, "NORMAL" people can get their VO2 Max levels into the great range. No excuses please! I have seen men in their seventies score in the excellent range for any age group. Yes, this does happen from time to time and older adults always seem to get a kick out of it. Admittedly, there is something amusing about watching a 75 year old grandfather, completely dominating a cocky youngster. As a side note, most rowers do not have VO2 Max levels as high as ultra-elite cyclists. This is due to rowers generally having greater body weights and this factor does decrease the score. Once weight is factored out, rowers score fairly high at around 6 liters/minute, with more elite rowers hitting 8 liters/minute. Please be careful here; rowers have a tendency to compare their scores with slimmer built endurance athletes and this should never be done! That being said, VO2 Max scores work just fine for larger rowers, at least when comparisons are made to other rowers with similar builds.

Typically, VO2 Max measurement is done one of three ways. The first is the real deal! If desired, pay a fee, go off to a sports science lab and have it done. This is the one typically done on a treadmill, with pinched nostrils and a hose hanging out of the mouth. These tests, while costing a few bucks, are more than worth it for the accuracy. If you have some extra cash, time and access to a sports lab, -the profession service can't be beat. The second method involves ways to estimate your VO2 Max. Such approaches rely not on lung gas measurements, but estimates based on how far you can run or step in a given time period. Almost all of these tests are measured differently, but they all get at the same thing. With the help of some cute equations containing age, sex and a few other variables, -fairly accurate estimates of VO2 Max can be made. These tests come in handy, as they can be repeated and compared against older tests to show improvement. The only items needed for such testing are a stop watch and in some cases, a way to measure distance. The third way to measure VO2 Max is by making estimates based on maximum heart rate. Through some strong analysis, a relationship between MHR and V02 Max was found. All that is needed for this method is a heart rate monitor. In many ways, this method is similar to the second, with the estimation coming via more abstracted means.

Honestly, no happiness can be had with any of these methods. Such methodologies range from annoyingly difficult, to somewhat quirky. There has to be a straight forward and relatively effortless way to obtain good VO2 Max readings! And as things would have it, there is. Ohio University's Dr. Hagerman came up with a simple method for obtaining virtually error free (~1%) VO2 Max scores by utilizing the Concept2. Using an online calculator, participants plug in their best 2k time, body weight, gender, training level and then, with nothing more than a c-l-i-c-k, an accurate VO2 Max measurement is spit out. How simple is that! All that is really needed is the best 2k time and the VO2 Max calculator does the rest. To say your author is exceedingly pleased with this method would be an under-statement. The easiest way to locate the calculator is by going to con-cept2.com and doing a search for **VO2Max calculator**. Strong ex-pectations can be made for other rowing machine manufacturers to follow Dr. Hagerman's example with the Concept2. In ending, take this super close approximation and run with it. The awkward breath-ing hoses can be left for the bikers and runners. Given the ease of this method, not to mention the ~1% error rate, -nothing much is left to complain about.

The next question is what to do with this number once it is ob-tained. The finalized VO2Max numeric is not some magical value that tells a participant to increase or decrease it and then to expect success. However, it does provide further insight and certain assump-tions, along with educated experiments can be carried out to aid the rower. For example, if it is a little low side, this may be an indication for the rower to increase the damper setting and see if that increases competitive times. After all, some athletes are naturally geared this way (more power & less total endurance). On the other had, perhaps the settings are fine and what really needs attention is losing some body fat and continually working to increase stamina. Likewise, if the initial VO2 Max reading is a little on the high side, this may be an indication to lower the damper setting in an effort to obtain faster times. Conversely, this may be an indication for any given athlete be-ing in need of more anaerobic training for any given distance (assum-ing shorter). A little detective work and some experimentation will go a long way. Additionally, V02 Max levels can be compared against other rowers, but be careful here, -there is no such thing as a perfect V02 Max score (the damper assures this) and as mentioned before, there is a weight bias. Comparisons have value, but please, treat them with caution.

Chapter 11

Rowing With Company

Given that rowing machines are designed for singular usage (excluding slides), not to mention their placement in hidden away areas, -isolation becomes more of the norm, than the exception. While such isolation is undoubtedly an attribute and a great boon to people wanting to blaze through workouts, -there are times when more is merrier and joining a rowing organization, or at the very least, getting together with other rowers, can really energize the experience. Many rowers find their rowing times drastically improving while engaging in group rowing. People tend to feed off the energy of others and some humans need competition/companionship to excel not only at rowing, but at anything they do. Unless you're a separatist, it's really a good idea to hook-up fellow rowers. For the most part, it is just human nature to desire grouping!

Once a machine has been acquired, take a few weeks to get in the swing of a good routine. Generally speaking, recommendations for group rowing cannot be made until the end of a few months or at the very least, a few weeks. There is a need for rowers to pass through a trial period to see what level of rowing can be handled without becoming overly fatigued. Once rowers get an idea as to what level can be safely handled and maintained, rowing with others can be sought out, but there is an alternative to face-to-face contact.

As we speak, various proprietary and independent computer programs are being written and refined for "real time" racing over the Net. The current trend seems to be centered around new racing software being designed in somewhat of a video game style. Functional programs depicting competitors, along with natural scenery, serve as a much needed boost for what is sometimes a visually bland sport. Nothing beats true person to person training or competition, but when none is available, -no better option is to be had. Let's face it, in these hectic days, people are not always available and in such situations, the Net really comes in handy. The Net never suffers from attendance problems. When it comes to software, vast differences in development can be seen between the various companies. If online racing/training is extremely important to you, a little due diligence is highly recommended! With that said, software changes in the blink of an eye and for that reason alone, taking a stab at software reviews, or time-stamping winners and losers makes no sense whatsoever. Research into current software offerings will have to be done right before the purchase. Networked programs aside, the Internet also puts forth less technologically sophisticated offerings such as online rankings. With such rankings, participants can get a feel as to where they stand in relation to age, sex and their times in general. Sticking a spreadsheet on the web is not the most complicated matter in computer science, but for those gearing-up for competition, these listings provide the only real dependable data for competitive rankings; in this regard, they are extremely valuable.

Adding to the fun, Concept2 offers something called a slide(s). To truly understand how slides work, they have to seen in action. A "slide" is a track that can be attached under a Concept2 machine in order to mimic the sensation of real water rowing. While in the water, the feeling of rowing is very different from that of the standard indoor motion. The true genius behind the slide(s) is not so much the real water simulation, but rather, being able to link-up two machines (or more) and in effect, become one machine. In other words, they give the experience of having another person(s) in a boat with you, with the added bonus of kinetic linkage. You and your partner(s) can perfectly synchronize movement and row as a team. And yes, yes, yes, the movement of one machine is linked to that of another; this "synchronization" is not faked! This invention, however much utilized, is probably one of the best gizmos in the history of the sport! It's simple, it works and rowers can now train with their significant other or training partner(s). Video of this device is available on the Concept2's web site. If you're interested in getting another machine or rowing with a partner, -check out the Concept2 slides. And again, they must be seen in action to be understood.

Rudeness is a horrible thing! When people visit, let them get on the machine and give rowing a try. The vast majority of humans have never ridden an indoor rowing machine and most people will never do so without being invited. Nothing can be lost by doing so! The machine cannot be broken and wearing one out is all but impossible. Unless time is taken to give a demo, the people around you will never learn to row; Again, most people have never been exposed to rowing! In fact, indoor rowing's exposure rate has been dismal to say the least; As to why this has been the case for so long is not always understood.

For many years, rowing (on the water) was exclusively the domain of European and American Ivy League universities and only practiced in locations with suitable river systems. For one reason or another, rowing's forefathers never managed to invent the 25 man boat, which obviously led to diminutive team sizes. The general populous has always had problems identifying with sports having small team numbers. If the full chess board is not set up, they never blink an eye. Higher head counts create greater variance, which allows for deeper analysis; after all, the statistical complexity is increased with every additional body. In the end, it allows for a more elaborate show for both the spectators and speculators. Indoor rowing was spawn of its aquatic parent and as can be seen, big daddy was not exactly popular. That being said, positive changes are occurring. Indoor rowing has now become a sport of its own and has begun to leave the umbrella of its water-based parent. Unfortunately, the formation of this fork is not occurring with any great speed. It would behoove the "indoor" community to engage in a little self-promotion. For those having already purchased a machine, do yourself and the sport a much needed favor; encourage people to get on and take a ride. As long as people never take that first ride, participation numbers will remain low and indoor rowing will always be looked upon as being rather peculiar.

As further involvement in the rowing community takes hold, a word of caution must be given. Most of rowing's hard-core fanatics are wonderful people to say the least. Generally speaking, lovers of this sport tend to find themselves in the "MORE" category. More giving, more down to earth, more intelligent and coming in with a "more" centralized level of thinking when it comes to family, friends and the community at large; undoubtedly, these are all true. With that said, a few bad apples occupy every bunch. Certain rowers have the singular ambition to physically dominate and humiliate all who cross their paths. These rowers are perhaps the sickest and most devious in the sport and they do exist. Rowing is a somewhat strange endeavor when consideration is given to its upper echelons; high level rowing equates to extreme pain and suffering. Watching someone suffer as they're being dominated, serves as a double bonus for these sadistic little creatures. Concerns for health, friendship and good/clean competition, always remain subordinate to the desire of domination. When encountering such types, be certain to give them no comfort, or for that matter, any attention whatsoever. Such "commentary" may seem a bit infantile and while these people bear no familiarity to more psychopathic among us, their ability to cause irritation grants them an honorable mention. Keep them out of your group and out of your life.

We next move onto major large scale major competitions. At this point in time, indoor rowing can now be classified a legitimate competitive sport. While early competitions were pocket-sized, yearly repetition did allow for the building of sizable, stable base. From this stable base, growth would further increase into what would become large scale competitive venues; in the U.S., the most notable being the annual CRASH-B, which has now become one of the most recognized worldwide rowing competitions. CRASH-B, while large in size, allows (as it always has) for admittance of the general public and with this non-exclusionary approach, a righteous "for the people vibe" is more than dominant. No effort is made for closed profession-al events, elitists sub-competitions, or any other invite-only competi-tions. This openness and friendliness to the community has done more for the sport than any other factor. Rowers, regardless of status, -whether it be world class or rookie, receive no advantage or restric-tion. Yes, anyone can go and compete with the best in the world. Very few competitive sports operate in this fashion! This is one for-mula which should be strictly monitored to avoid any change. When ordinary people can compete side-by-side with the "greats," can any-thing other than a complete lack of arrogance be assumed? Try doing this with football, baseball, basketball, hockey, golf and so on; there is always a "wall" with these sports; indoor rowing has no wall! As of this writing, ~20 bucks is the admittance fee and non-competitors are welcome. You can expect to see such events held in arena style settings with the added visual effect of what appears to be a massive cloning experiment with Concept2 machines. Each machine is net-worked to a central computer and from there, into a large central display. Bar graphs (currently depicted as little boats) on the large screen denote a rower's progress along with all other competitors for any given race. It is similar to watching horse racing, only much slower. High recommendations can be given for anyone fit enough to compete. It is not as serious as most would assume. Don't worry, large numbers of amateurs attend CRASH-B just have to fun and to get in a little racing experience. So no fretting if you come in ugh, -whatever place you happen to come in. For those desiring more information on CRASH-B world rowing championships, please visit: http://www.crash-b.org.

For those on the other side of the pond, Britain plays host to the largest rowing championships in the world. The British Indoor Rowing Championships (BIRC) are basically the same as CRASH-B competitions, only with with a European twist. As with almost all competitive venues, BIRC exclusively uses the Concept2 rowing machine. If it hasn't become apparent by now, those wishing to compete in large scale competitions are pretty much locked in to buying a Concept2 rower. Concept2 seems to have a complete monopoly in this area and as a side note, BIRC is in fact organized by Concept2. No anger is to be had, -the people at Concept2 have more than earned the trust of the rowing community. Their products are well engineered and affordable. As long as these traditions are maintained, there is nothing to complain about. More information on BIRC can be found at: http://www.concept2.co.uk/birc/

Last but not least, there is no rule which says you cannot actually go out on the water. If you're lucky enough to live near a suitable water system, there is most certainly a club in your area which goes out on the water. These clubs are generally more than happy to teach you all the technical details of rowing on the water. If going this route, up-to-par swimming skills are a must. All rowers wishing to go out on the water should be able to effectively swim and tread water for an extended period of time (20 minutes) with additional weight. While rowing on the water, life vests are usually not worn! And for Pete's sake, make sure you are with people who know what they are doing. The water is being shared with other boaters, barges, damns and a ton of other things which can get you into serious trouble. Essentially, you are out-gunned while on the water. Everything is either larger than you or more powerful than you and it would be wise to keep this simple fact in mind. Experienced rowers will keep you safe, dry and out of trouble. Make certain they are experienced!

Chapter 12

Successful Competitive Training

For competition purposes, we begin with the "training wheels " routine for two months. These races are not to be taken too seriously, but at the same time, are not to be laughed off. This is the ramping-up process to get competitors used to rowing the full 2,000 meters. Competitors who row at 100% intensity, day-after-day, typically burn out very quickly. This "training wheels" routine addresses the issue and slightly decreases full racing intensity. Allowances are also made for vacation days; use them as suggested! The workout is as follows:

Training Wheels Routine -Two Months Duration

Monday   2,000 meters 85-90%
Tuesday   2,000 meters 85-90%
Wednesday Off-day/just relax, nothing else

Thursday	2,000 meters 85-90%
Friday	Off-day/just relax, nothing else
Saturday	Race day... full 2,000 meters at 100%
Sunday	Off-day/just relax, nothing else

It is a fabulous little workout, which provides plenty of racing experience with the addition of a real (100% effort) Saturday race. Regarding all other training days, the given percentages of 85%-90%, pertains to any athletes maximum. A test race at 100% should be done before these workouts begin; simply scale back from the finishing time. Despite not being at 100%, these training days will still be demanding; that is just the way it goes with the 2,000 meter event. This distance lends itself to difficulty even when maximum effort is not being put forth. The first Saturday race will be valuable in letting competitors know exactly where they stand. Now is a good time to look up online rankings and see how much, or how little work needs to done. Now is not the time for panic. Relax, there is plenty of time left. More than any other reason, these early races are for "experience only" and working out any kinks. Please continue this workout for two straight months. And please be mindful to reset the 85-90% pace time if a new record is achieved on any given Saturday race.

Backtracking a little, the reference to "kinks" is not always understood. Simple matters such as clothing have to be figured out during this time. Problems such as chaffing, long t-shirts getting stuck in the seat's wheels and little thought of problems such as sweat running into the eyes have to be solved. All of these kinks have to be addressed and rectified long before the competition starts. Is a 70's style headband needed for sweat? What kind of shorts are going to be worn? Are wrestling style singlets more comfortable than synthetic biker shorts? Does your butt slip off the seat after long periods of rowing? Is it the fabric creating the slip, or is it bad form? During competition, taking two extra seconds to wipe sweat from the eyes is a big NO-NO. This is competition and every second counts! Likewise, you don't want to stop rowing and engage in some weird "reposition wiggle" to get your butt back in the center of the seat. This is your time to get things figured out and to get comfortable with the 2,000 meter distance. On race day, everything should seem familiar. No surprises! It is time to shift gears and start looking at what will be our final training cycle.

The Final 2 Month Competitive Training

Entrance into the competitive sphere changes just about everything. The functionality, general health (excluding acute/serious problems) and architectural beauty of the body no longer warrant any concern whatsoever. Hardcore competition training is about one thing and one thing only, -winning. How such "winning" should be achieved is the great question. Higher adaptation is the obvious answer, but with so many options at hand, picking a correct methodology remains daunting. Other forms of exercise, such as stair climbing could be used, but these would be counterproductive. With rowing, the legs are being used in tandem and the motion itself is exceedingly unique. Other activities will do little more than condition the muscles away from optimal rowing performance. In almost all case, far too much weight is placed on the legs and given activities do little to properly mimic rowing's unique compound movement; in the end, nothing more than a double fault is to be had. I've seen people doing split-knee squats for better rowing performance, leg presses, running, high repetition clean n' jerk movements, roman-chair exercises, the aforementioned stair climbing, along with a whole host of others. None of it works! Training for greater adaptation must be exclusively done on the indoor rowing machine!

Still yet, ushering in this new adaptation remains tricky. Regardless of the participant's motivation, rowing at faster levels cannot and will not be obtained past a certain point. It is almost as if the brain and body have built-in dead-bolts which lock down after a certain point and disallow further advancement. When such points are reached, increased stress has to be artificially placed upon the participant. It is no different that having someone exercise on a planet with a greater gravitational pull, or thinking more reasonably, training (on earth) at higher altitudes. Forced adaptation, by such means, leads to the development of superhuman levels of conditioning; absolutely no exaggeration is being made here. The same idea is directly applicable to indoor rowing. This is where the aforementioned "trickiness" comes in. Bright rowers who understand the negatives of non-specific muscular training and the "correctness" of machine-only training, always seem to gravitate towards machine tweaking for greater intensity. The first go-to solution (which everyone tries) is to change the machine settings for greater intensity. A major error is at hand and red flags should be shooting up everywhere. NO, NO, NO!

Changing the settings will force rowers to maintain a different stroke rate. If this is done for too long, correct rate-specific conditioning, along with the proper "feel" will be completely lost. This is the number one mistake made by rookies who are bright, but not bright enough to understand how easily strategic mishaps occur. The resistance of the rowing machine must never be changed from what produces optimal performance for the 2,000 meter race without any kind of added resistance. The other go-to strategy involves physical tweaks to the machine, or in some cases, even to the person. Ideas range from wearing backpacks with a few additional pounds, to slightly jacking-up the back-end of the machine in an effort to increase gravity's influence. All of these ideas do more harm than good.

Still yet, some form of resistance must be applied. The best single answer I have ever found is to use a simple house fan. Not anything inbuilt, but a normal stand alone fan that can be place directly behind the rower. Too simple to be true and yet, -the best answer anyone could ever hope for. As mentioned before, the problem with forcing higher adaptive stress upon any given rower comes about when too much resistance is used. The resistance should be incredibly small and occur all the way throughout the rowing session. This is exactly what the fan does and it doesn't mess with the machine! It gives a tiny bit of wind resistance for each and every stroke and while not major, the additive effect is more than apparent by the end of 2,000 meters. Its a perfect solution! A nice and gentle means of forcing adaptive stress. You could sit a baby elephant on your lap while training and crushingly cute as it may be, no benefits would be had for the 2,000 meter race.

Does adaptive rowing with the fan produce any problems? Truthfully speaking, there are NO real problems to be had with this technique. There are however a few small issues to discuss and anyone thinking the matter over, will quickly come to one stark conclusion. If the fan is making it harder on the drive, then it is making it easier on the recovery! Yes, yes, and yes, -this is true, but it does not matter. The majority of the work is being done on the drive and only a very limited amount is being done on the recovery. The helpful effect of the fan during the recovery is of minimal importance due to the small amount of energy needed to carry it out in the first place. There is **not** a 1:1 relationship between the drive and recovery. It is no different than having to run as fast as possible against the wind and then having to briskly walk back with the aid of the wind. Very little help is being given on the walk back, but man can it be felt when running against it. Another area of concern revolves around which fan to choose. Nothing crazy here, just a normal medium sized house fan, with blades averaging around 12 inches or so. Nothing too small and don't even consider those hyper-powerful industrial fans. No N.A.S.A. wind tunnels, -please! Medium should be the setting, -nothing more than a strong breeze. The only matter in need of discussion is the cooling effect produced by the fan. Having all that extra air whirling around does a lot to reduce the rower's temperature and serves to strongly reduce stress on the body. A desirable aid, but not one that will be available on race day. When utilizing fan training, long sleeve hooded shirts are a must. This is one piece of advice that should absolutely be headed. Think back in time and remember the difference between how much work could be done on a very hot/humid day verses a cool breezy day. The differences between the two are staggering. Total work load, along with intensity, can easily double or triple during cooler weather. Please head the advice and properly compensate for the cooling effect! Don't go overboard here and use thick sweatshirts, that would create too much heat. Something a little thinner.

This two month stage will be the last before competition, so relax, take a deep breath and maintain a focused mindset. The normal seven day training loop gets thrown out the window for a more efficacious 14 day loop. During this training phase, the stated goal is to become an alien in terms of ability; an alien that trains at a level which no real competition can be felt. The opposition is to be delightfully situated in a state of semi-permanent confusion. It should be no different than watching a chimpanzee reading a book on vector calculus; keep them scratching their heads. As far as they are concerned, your an unbeatable genetic freak of nature, or more appropriately stated, an alien. This is pretty much what were going for and if you've made it to this point, you're well on your way. And one final thought; please let there be no complaining about the aggressive posturing; competition is cold and winning at the game will require no less of a mindset. High level competition is a pressurized situation demanding nothing less than methodical preparation. You will want to be mentally and physically topped-off for this. This is how winning is achieved and this is where the fan comes in.

The workout is as follows:

Day 1 Row 2,000 with fan

Day 2 Off

Day 3 Row 2,000 with fan

Day 4 Off

Day 5 Row 2,000 with fan

Day 6 Off

Day 7 Row 2,000 with fan

Day 8 Off

Day 9 Row 2,000 with fan

Day 10 Off

Day 11 Row 2,000 with fan

*done in the morning to allow for for maximum rest before the day 14 race.

Day 12 Off (1 of 2 days off)

Day 13 Off (2 of 2 days off)

Day 14 Test Day – Row 2,000 meters without the fan

Anyone having done these workouts can attest to their grueling nature. And yes, even though the added fan resistance is of little consequence for each individual stroke, the added effect can really be felt by the end. Get ready for the pain; it is coming and you can't stop it. Rowing should now be done at 100% effort for each and every training day.

Without first being in exceedingly good shape and then engaging in the training wheels routine, -this workout schedule would be exceedingly difficult. Enough adaptation should have previously occurred to give a protective effect. That being said, these workouts will still be grueling. If any race distance receives massive complaints, its the 2,000 meter event. It is short enough to allow for enough speed to create acute pain and long enough to instill a burning, rusty sort of pain. Truly a cruel distance and when competitively paced, -allowing for the worst of both worlds. Rowing's upper echelons are not to be taken lightly. This is one of the most strenuous activities on the planet and with the added fan resistance, it only gets harder.

As far as the pain is concerned, every effort is made to get the body into a higher adaptive state to deal with such circumstances, but in the end, if you want to excel in advanced competition, swimming through rougher waters must be done. Some modern sport specialists will often say otherwise, but what they are alluding to is over-training/injury and not what may be termed "good pain." Notice again, needed pressuring is applied, but not to the point of over-training, or injury. While individual workouts are hard, multiple workouts per day are not prescribed, nor are there any back-to-back days of real rowing for that matter! Again, there is a difference between adaptive pain and pain coming from over-training or injury. Don't worry, you are not being throw into shark infested waters without protection; chapter 14 will give numerous adaptive strategies for athletes to utilize. Take advantage of them.

It's day 14, -time to turn the fan off and row a regular race without added wind resistance. It's an official race day and this test counts. Remember, this is a serious race and should be treated accordingly. Turn all the phones off and DO NOT allow for interruptions. Wear the appropriate clothing and record the results! Having two off days before the race was done for a reason. The extra recovery day will allow for additional reserves to build up. Again, this race is to be attacked with full force. After racing with the added fan resistance, the rowing movement should feel exceedingly light, almost as if cheating is occurring. This is good! The early stages of the race should feel somewhat effortless. This is what we have been working towards all along! The effect is similar to a baseball player swinging a bat with a doughnut; the only difference being the continuing application. And unlike the doughnut trick, the extra resistance is not some psychological trick to be used directly before competition, -this is real adaptation! If the rowing machine feels light, that's because it is. If rowing feels easier after five minutes, that's because it is. Rowing without the extra fan resistance should be little more than laughable! Remember, you are ahead of the game now. There is an advantage here; it is very real and measurable! Have No fear, No anxiety and certainly No doubt. This one is for real, give it your all!

There you have it for the first 14 days. With any luck, the winning time has already been reached. If not, you now know how much work needs to be done. Be patient, plenty of time is left. With each passing week, you should be honing your times. Does more work need to be done, or are you on point? With a little calculating and strategic thought, there should be no problems to speak of. At the end of this two month cycle, one last race before competition day is to be had. Again, give this one everything you got and I mean everything. It's almost competition time.

At this point, a little strategy is to be employed. You are going to take a five to ten day vacation right before the race. No joke is being made here. Absolutely nothing but rest and relaxation. Four months of total training has been done up to this point, -with the last two being excruciating. Giving your body a set time for recovery is the proper thing to do. Everything from the muscles to the red blood cells will receive an extra boost. This five-ten day break will come as a very welcome rest and will serve as the last factor for ensuring success. As for the variance in rest days, this is easy to see; in most cases, a 22 year old will not need as much recovery time as a 72 year old. Total days can be added or subtracted as needed. The idea is to give as much rest as is needed and supercharge the body right before the race. Many hopeful competitors do the worst possible thing and train right up until competition day. As a result, they come in depleted and spent. For them, all the hard work was in vain. Don't be surprised if you find yourself crushing your own personal best after this break. You will want to massage yourself frequently and do some light stretching during this rest period, but that's about it! If competing with a heart rate monitor, don't be surprised if your heart rate is lower than it was previously when doing the same amount of work. However, this may not actually happen if you are a little high-strung on competition day. Having so many rowers in one room, not to mention the observational stress, can be unnerving; Your resting heart rate may be reflective of this fact. That being said, some people are more affected by situational stress than others. Be sure to set your training cycle back five-ten days to accommodate the rest period.

Final Thoughts on Race Day

With five-ten days of rest being given, you should be very fresh, almost bouncing off the walls fresh. There are a few things to re-member on race day. Don't eat a big meal before the race and don't eat meat. Meat especially, takes too long to digest. Having all that blood in your stomach, when it should be in your legs/arms, is forbid-den. The steak can be eaten the night before and that's fine, but not on game day. In general, it's a good idea to come equipped with some energy bars. What great little inventions! They provide enough cal-ories to keep the hunger away, but are not large enough, or heavy enough to bog you down. Along with a few energy bars, some Gato-rade or a similar energy drink is also a good idea. Additionally, con-sume some caffeine before racing. I like tea myself, but if coffee is your thing, be my guest. Coffee and tea are good choices, but a Coke or two is the absolute best thing. Sound crazy? It's not and just be-cause soft drinks have gotten a bad rap, -that doesn't mean they don't work, especially in competitive settings. Large amounts of sugar + fairly high concentrations of caffeine are an absolutely perfect com-bination. You might be surprised to find out how many endurance athletes (especially bikers) swear by this practice. Unbelievable as it sounds, Coke is a much revered sports drink! If taking a Coke or two before rowing, allow it to go flat before drinking; gaseous problems (burping) are to be avoided. While not a prescription for daily use, a

Coke or two before racing is just what the doctor ordered. The only contradiction is for those who are unaccustomed, or overly sensitive to caffeine.

Stretching is another good suggestion for some pre-race performance enhancement. This stretching, while seemingly nothing more than a generalized warm-up, is utilized for a very specific purpose. Stretching, more than any other activity, helps the body to coordinate movement. Better coordination leads to better efficiency and thus, faster times. Increased coordination between the catch, drive and recovery will add up to more than most would think and every second counts when it comes to international competition. It will all be cleaner and "cleaner" equates to speed. You can have a lot of power, but if your body is not coordinating muscular contractions in a proper time-linked fashion, you won't be standing on the podium. Try 30-45 minutes of total body stretching before going to the race. To add to this effect, you are also going to give yourself a massage before the race in the hotel room or wherever you are staying. Lastly, before getting on the rower for the race, briskly rub or slap the muscles. This "stimulation" helps wake the muscles up. Anyone having watched sprinters, should be familiar with this practice.

What about the large mega-screen(s) showing all the competitors progress? Well, don't look up at them. You are already aware of what time needs to be beaten, so don't worry about it. Glancing at the mega-screen has been known to induce panic in some people. As with any group, some fool always goes off on a mad dash at the beginning and those susceptible to knee-jerk reactions, may become roused and start sprinting themselves. Mad dashes at the beginning only lead to lost time in the end. Stick with the game plan and row your race. You should know exactly what time needs to be beaten at 500 meters, 1,000 meters, 1,500 meters and so on. There is no guess-work here and coaches are completely unnecessary; the monitor is the best coach anyone could ever ask for. With all of your training, everyone should be following you. So don't worry about the big screen. Sometimes rowers are not even in a position to see it and that's a good thing.

It's race day! GO, --Good luck, relax and have fun!

Chapter 13

Future Competitive Training

So what now, the competition is over and done with. Hopefully everything went well and your looking forward to years and years of competition. Throughout the previous training, four total months of training was given, plus five to ten days of rest before the competition. Is this how the next year should be treated? The answer is no. Using the exact same training regimen would be fine, but changing things up a bit can add for some additional gains. The total time will only be a month longer, but remember, smart athletes stay in shape all year round. Smart athletes are also sure to take a nice long rest in between competitions.

Up to this point, indirect competition training was never spoken of and there was a reason for it. Anyone reading this book would probably not have enough time, or more importantly, the patience to engage in it. The idea is to get one competition under the belt with simple training and leave indirect training for the next go around.

So what is indirect training? It is not primary training, that is for sure. The previous four month training schedule was the primary training. Indirect training keys in on the same philosophy as the fan training. Fan training was implemented due to the body's eventual refusal to row faster under standard training conditions. This was spoken of as a "deadbolt" problem. With indirect training, a very slick training practice is going to be adopted from the world of cycling. This training practice has no basis in rowing and lacks any official name; it will simply be referred to as high-low training. With high-low training, the idea is to create a hybrid by doing speed training and then longer endurance training (not super long). By doing both, the middle distance (2,000) will be magically maximized. As was described previously, rowing uses both fast twitch and slow twitch muscle fibers, however, the varying percentages are of little concern in this case. With high-low training, all that needs to be given attention is the total distance (2,000 meters) and the corresponding high and low cuts. Rowers will do 1,000 meter sprints (relatively speaking), along with longer 3,000 meter races. By maximizing both speed and distance, a beautiful supercharged hybrid is created for the 2,000 meter race. The indirect workout (high-low) is as follows:

For three months duration:

Day 1 1,000 meter sprint

Day 2 1,000 meter sprint

Day 3 off

Day 4 3,000 meter endurance

Day 5 3,000 meter endurance

Day 6 off

Day 7 2,000 meter race

That is it, nice and simple! Continue this phase for three months. Please notice, the training wheels program is cut out of the equation. After three months, please transition into the fan training.

For 2 months duration:

Day 1 Row 2,000 with fan

Day 2 Off

Day 3 Row 2,000 with fan

Day 4 Off

Day 5 Row 2,000 with fan

Day 6 Off

Day 7 Row 2,000 with fan

Day 8 Off

Day 9 Row 2,000 with fan

Day 10 Off

Day 11 Row 2,000 with fan *done in the morning to allow for maximum rest before the day 14 race.

Day 12 Off (1 of 2 days off)

Day 13 Off (2 of 2 days off)

Day 14 Test Day – Row 2,000 meters without the fan

* don't forget the five to ten vacation days off at the end of two months

Please note, only five total months of training have been given. As to what what should be done for the rest of the year is a personal choice. Do whatever is desired, but stay in shape and continue rowing. You can use any of the previously prescribed training regimes (non-competitive), sprints, longer races (not too long), or just the standard 2,000 meter races. Feel free to do whatever comes to mind before the set training period begins. When the calender reads five months (plus vacation days) before the competition, it is time to get back on track with the written schedule; playtime is over! The schedule is there for a reason. Utilizing the high-low program with fan resistance training is as good as can be hoped for. No, actually, its better, -bordering on superb. The early indirect workout allows for the creation of a super hybrid, while the last two months of fan training hone the blade to a razors edge; this is what is known as escalated training, where one advancement is obtained and further built upon. Anyone lacking knowledge of these techniques will be shocked to see the numbers thrown down by rowers using them. Rowers using these techniques may well be accused of using performance enhancing drugs! What a beautiful complement.

Chapter 14

Competitive Adaptive Strategies

When it comes to competition, proper adaptation is the key. Adaptive ability is directly linked to the healing response. The capacity of the healing response must be increased and this is one factor which is not always given proper consideration. Increasing performance by way of certain training procedures is often given focus, but healing capacity and its corresponding effect on performance is almost never given attention. Healing is everything when it comes to increasing athletic performance. The best training systems in the world could be utilized, which would correctly apply positive adaptive stress, while simultaneously avoiding over training, but without a good healing capacity, very little in the way of advancement would be made. This "enhanced healing" becomes critically important when competitive training begins. Under such conditions, the body is facing exceedingly high amounts of wear n' tear and only enhanced healing will allow for significant improvements from workout to workout. Every athlete undergoing competitive training is highly encouraged to adopt many, if not all of the following adaptive techniques. Doing so will give a massive advantage over the pact.

Calm Water

Psychological stress is common issue for which proper attention should be given. Typically speaking, this is topic which most people will want to avoid. During this training cycle, take care to distance yourself from personal turmoil, -especially in relationships. Screaming matches over "this-and-that" are strictly forbidden! Either work it out or move on, but at no time can you subject yourself to such craziness. It's funny as to how much psychological stress can screw up the body. Show me an angry person who says they sleep well and I'll show you a liar. Show me an agitated person who says they heal well and I'll show you a liar. Show me a jealous person who says they can concentrate heavily and I'll show you a liar. The point here is isn't to take a stab at cleverness, but for acknowledgment of the mind/body relationship and more importantly, for emphasis to be placed on maintaining a happy, healthy and relaxed mind. Stay away from angry situations, confrontations, or for that matter, any other forms of distress which can, could, may, or might lead to exceedingly high levels of psychological tension. Doing so will allow for better sleep, faster recovery, enhanced immune system function and will result in other seldom appreciated factors, such as feeling less physical pain.

As is sometimes the case, the least of which, or specifically the later in this case, might prove to be exceeding important during competition; perhaps a little hint was just given!

Those waiting for the speech on the ten steps to proper psychological health shouldn't get their hopes up. No specifics will be given; everyone is different and has varying needs, not to mention situational factors. That being said, take care to do simple things which are fun and enjoyable. Movies, restaurants, games and whatever else is simple, -yet fun. In other words, don't make the entire scope of life about training and the never ending road of achievement. Make the mistake of having "this" 24/7 always-on mentality and an irritable, burned-out state will take hold faster than you or anybody else could possibly imagine. Most people have a somewhat disquieted attitude when it comes to the topic of psychology and understandably maintain a certain amount of animosity for society's oh-so beloved, "know-it-all" armchair shrinks. Obviously, there are one too many of these "types" running around the planet. Most of these pseudo-shrinks have less than stellar lives, but still yet, maintain a compulsive drive to give others advice; this new practice has become the gold standard in passive aggressive behavior. A vexing situation at best! Despite the annoyances brought forth by these depraved little cretins, the importance of psychological heath and its effects on human performance are in no way diminished. It has been shown, time and time again, that good psychological health is strongly measurable in the physical sphere and everybody should strive for it. You have been advised and no more shall be said.

Massage

While the nurturing of proper cognitive function cannot be understated, using more simplistic means to modulate physical and mental systems is oftentimes far more efficacious; this is where massage comes in. In our modernistic age, massage is not only undervalued, but oftentimes passed off as irrelevant, or worse yet, viewed as somewhat of a snake oil treatment. Despite the simplicity and ancient origins of this treatment, massage remains one of the most beneficial health practices available. And this remains true, even when stacked against the modern advances of medicine, training and nutrition. In fact, it is probably one of the greatest therapeutic treatments known to man. Massage results in the following: Increased bone strength, improved joint health, increased tissue elasticity/flexibility, blood vessel dilation, increased skin health, muscular relaxation, toxin removal, enhanced nervous system function, natural pain killer enhancement (increased mood, decreased pain), increased red blood cell counts (when needed), increased muscular nutrition, improved sleep, improved immune system function, increased concentration, scar tissue elimination, decreased muscular decay (for those inactive), partial mimicry of exercise (exercise replacement when none is available), increased rates of intestinal evacuation, increased fat burning (yes, despite the arguments and controversy, this does happen to some degree), decreased breathing rates and deepening of breathing. Please, go right ahead, -take the challenge of finding any drug which can mimic all of these effects. It doesn't exist, but if it did, how much would people pay for it? The effects of frequent massage are outstanding to say the least, but in most cases, application is done in a faulty manner. Let's be honest, most people do not ever receive massages and even for those partaking, it's generally on an intermittent basis. Massaging the body on an intermittent basis does nothing to improve general health. Adding to the problem, massage is often applied to injured areas, which only furthers the damage. Increased tearing and bleeding are not exactly desirable, but that is exactly what is happening. Acute problems resulting from excessive strain are in need of ice, not massage. And massage should never be applied to diseased tissue. Please, healthy tissue only! For massage to be effective, it has to be carried out on a daily basis.

For good results, application should be done every day for a month's duration, followed by the skipping of a month and then repeating. In other words, you should be getting massaged for six months out of a year and this is best done by someone else. If you are lucky enough to have this "someone else" lending a helping had, then make sure daily application is available. Fat chance you say? Welcome to reality, only highly paid athletes have the luxury of professional masseuses, -willing and available for daily rub-downs. Luckily, there is a better option by way of electrical massagers. Spend your money wisely and stick with the high-end models. As an added benefit, these massagers can produce vibrational rates which are nearly impossible to duplicate with human hands. The only cautionary note is to stay away from ultra-fast/ultra-hard settings. Remember, what can help in moderation, can hurt in excess and massage is certainly no different in this regard. Ultra-fast/ultra-hard vibrational rates can do more harm than good. Keep the vibrational rate fairly gentle and allow yourself to do most of the work.

The initial effects of massage will generally be perceivable after several days of continual application. Suddenly, your body will recover faster from exercise and with less soreness; this alone, is highly valuable for any competitor. Additionally, enhancements in sleep will be felt, along with slight reductions in stress. Enhanced relaxation, with less of a tendency to react negatively, along with the other significant physical enhancements, provide for positive feedback during the early going. And after a few months of application, a generalized upswing in health, strength and endurance will be felt. **In the end, this is one practice which should come with easy adoption**. Considering the ease, cost and enjoyment factor, -no better adjunctive aid could be given.

Ice Therapy

Ice therapy helps the body heal faster after exercise. The cold stops hemorrhaging and reduces cellular death. Nothing much is going on here that people don't already know about. After all, ice therapy is not exactly new. It works, it's cheap and despite being one of the best healing modalities, barely anybody uses it. Professional athletes do, but that is about it. Long diatribes on techniques such as RICE will not be given. Here is the simple procedure: After each and every workout during the final two months of training, ice packs should be used on the legs, back, shoulders and arms. Use two packs at time and keep them applied for a long enough time to create a slight numbing sensation. If ice therapy is undesirable for any reason, there is a good secondary option; learn to take cold showers. While delivering a slightly attenuated effect, they do help out. The choice is yours, pick one or the other, but learn to chill the body after exercise and please, don't ever use ice before exercising; that is a recipe for disaster.

A Discussion of Laziness

Ah, -and here we have the sinful sloth. A pathetic creature, with little self-respect and a massive appetite for nothingness. It is true, nothing favorable can be said of this slow and indolent creature. It is time for a little reality check! The work output of any given athlete is massive compared to that of sedentary person. Allowing certain days, or certain segments of days for rest may be sinful for some, but not for a competitive athlete. Here is a little secret which no workaholic will ever admit to. When more rest is given, greater work output can be obtained. Recovery from hard-core competitive training is no different. During the last stage of competitive rowing, alternating days are taken off for a reason. This recovery is IMPORTANT, -so be sure to use the rest days as suggested. No exercise at all; just sit around and be lazy. Yeah, I said it, just be lazy. Rent some movies, get some popcorn, invite some friends over and just relax. Whatever you do, don't go and help someone move into a new house. Don't go out and do yard work and don't engage in any sports if asked. Just vegetate and catch up on some reading. That's it!

Overfeeding, the Great Miracle

Many have wondered if there is anything that can be done to gain a sizable advantage on race day. After all, everyone wants an edge. This simple desire for an "edge" often leads many competitors into dangerous waters, -pressing some to look for advantages that are not exactly legal. Is there a safe/legal/morally correct technique which can be done to have a significant impact on race day performance? There is one hardcore effect which can be shared.

In the late 90's, a strange and surprising breakthrough came about. Bill Phillips of Muscle Media 2000 Magazine started reporting on some interesting findings by a man named Torbjorn Akerfeldt. At the time, Mr. Akerfeldt was studying Medicine at Uppsala University in Sweden. It would seem that he developed a new theory. Actually, it was not much of a theory, but more of a fact. With a little help from prior research, he would crack one of the more interesting bio-chemical puzzles. Reflecting back on the past 30 years exercise, it is pretty obvious that athletes figured out the bulk of needed knowledge. The only focused areas of research were in supplementation and without question, that once red hot industry was starting to cool. Past a certain point of development, there can only be so many momentous discoveries per decade and two or three seems to be the cap. With every passing decade, it gets harder and harder to unearth anything new, -at least in terms of substantial discovery. Out of these boring dregs came a colossal discovery and it had nothing to do with supplementation. Too simple to be true and far too massive to be overlooked.

Mr. Akerfeldt came onto the scene talking about a program called Anabolic burst cycling; the full name of this regimen is Anabolic Burst Cycling Diet and Exercise or (ABCDE) for short. Essentially, this diet regimen consists of repeated cycles of strict caloric reduction (two weeks), followed by two weeks of heavy overfeeding. Why would anybody follow this diet? Well, the body will produce a massive increase in anabolic hormones when overfed.[3] Levels of anabolic hormones will roughly double during this 14 day period of gluttony. If curious, the peak in hormone production occurs right at the very end of the 14 day overfeeding cycle. If the overfeeding cycle goes in excess of two weeks, the body starts becoming inefficient at handling the extra calories and begins storing them as fat. This is exactly when the overfeeding cycle is halted and the participant jumps back down to 14 days of dieting. From here, the cycle just continues on-and-on. This naturally occurring stack of anabolic hormones from overfeeding is thought to be one of the most powerful growth stimulating cocktails known to man. As many have rightfully theorized, this natural stack may even work better than some performance enhancing drugs when isolated in-and-of themselves. In a nutshell, this discovery serves as a natural way to achieve a chemical medley only seen during puberty. This is powerful!

They next question is obvious; what can be expected on this diet, in terms of gains? Well, it was designed for bodybuilders to build lean mass and it accomplishes this goal quite nicely. During the 14 days of overfeeding, participants can expect to gain anywhere from three to seven pounds of weight. The muscle to fat ratio of the newly gained weight is roughly 2:1 during this period. Not bad, so if six pounds of weight are gained, approximately two pounds will be fat and the rest will be muscle. Here is where things get interesting. When in the dieting phase, you'll burn more fat than muscle mass; the body does so preferentially when dieting! The relationship is this case is reversed. The muscle loss to fat loss ratio for the diet phase is 1:2. With some simple math, you can see a continued cycle of muscle gain, with almost no net increase in fat levels. After all, if you're always gaining more muscle than fat and always losing more fat than muscle, this can't be anything other than amazing in terms of gains in lean muscularity.

People who have followed the ABCDE regimen have described the overfeeding phase as being in a state of ever increasing energy. Most of the time, after doing strenuous workouts, people are completely spent for the next day or two and sometimes this PAIN n' DRAIN phase can last up to five days. Not on the overfeeding cycle! Dramatic increases in strength will be felt, along with the feeling of limitless energy reserves. This effect occurs even when highly intense, back-to-back workouts are done; to call this amazing would be an understatement. Ever increasing hormones + large amounts of fuel = the perfect anabolic environment not only for building muscle, but also for increased recovery times.

After the overfeeding phase, a couple of pounds of muscle, along with a little fat will be gained, but again, to a lesser degree with the fat. It's important to remember, if we were to continue overeating past 14 days, the results would be disastrous. Again, the body will stop making more muscle than fat and store the excess calories mainly as fat. The body has feedback loops which control these sorts of things and tricking them (for more than two weeks) can be very difficult, if not impossible in most cases. After 14 days of overeating, participants move into the dieting phase!

Next comes the nightmare phase of the program. After 14 days of joyous gluttony, we descend into the hell of caloric restriction. Caloric restriction is never fun, but caloric restriction after overfeeding is horrid. You will feel tired and have low energy levels. Additionally, you will be as irritated as they get. Doctors have a name for this condition and it's called malaise. None of the symptoms will be specific, but you will be keenly aware of the irritability, agitation low energy levels and what the shrinks call "decreased vigilance." The effects are not exactly subtle. Having low blood sugar levels is one of the more uncomfortable feelings for a human. All of us, by nature, were designed to become nasty and agitated when hungry. Many of our ancestors unfortunately starved to death and this fact was not lost in our genetic programming. That being said, agitation in regard to low blood sugar is not the same for everyone. Different people have varying levels at which they will start to feel the effects of low blood sugar. Yes, two people can have the exact same blood sugar levels and have different reactions. One person may feel fine when moving into a state of low blood sugar and another person, at the exact same level, may start to get moody, irritable and develop shaky hands. Eventually, even the resistant person will start to feel the effects, but it might take him or her another ten point drop to start feeling it.

Without question, this diet phase is harsh, but it is needed to shed off the small amount of fat gained during the overfeeding phase. More importantly, it is needed to prime the body for the next overfeeding phase. You have to admit, this regimen, however difficult, is creative in terms of how it activates the body's inbuilt signal for enhanced hormonal production, all the while, still adhering to the body's own regulatory mechanisms. It is incredibly clever!

The initial reporting by Bill Phillips on ABCDE set off a firestorm of interest not only in the bodybuilding community, but throughout the entire fitness community. Early adherents of ABCDE were reporting back with glowing results and it wasn't long before even the most ardent of critics were backpedaling. Nothing much can be said when something just works. The only thing left to question was whether the body would become privy (adaptively speaking) to what was going on over a course of a few months and stop releasing such high hormone levels down the road. Also, various experts had expressed concerns of the body reaching a point of maximum muscularity, whereby the body would eventually refuse to gain muscle past a certain point. By their logic, such a regimen may become pointless after eight months or so. Unfortunately, both of these questions have yet to be fully answered. What we do know is that it works in the short run and works well!

After everything was said and done, the ABCDE program was a huge failure. Almost nobody in the bodybuilding community used it for any length of time. Why you ask? -Oh, it's not what you're thinking; the diet does in fact work. The real problem revolved around the lack of maintainability and the general difficulty of the program. People tend to enjoy having fixed schedules. They like getting up and eating at regular times, doing certain exercises on certain days and keeping regular periods for recovery. Let's face it, people love fixed schedules along with permanently fixed meal sizes. Don't get me wrong, a little spice is nice, but concerning "ease of living," humans demand repetition in almost all daily tasks. This repetition allows the mind to be placed in a low energy consuming mode and frees up needed reserves for novel tasks. This "autopilot" for the mind is essential for anyone expecting reasonable levels of productivity in modern day society. It may sounds trivial, but spending major amounts of time figuring dieting schedules, portions and correct food choices, is more than most people can handle. There is a reason why some of the greatest minds had a love for routine and an utter disdain for trivial matters leading to distraction.

Problems with unfamiliarity aside, the ABCDE program's greatest defect comes by way of its daunting caloric restriction. This notion of overfeeding yourself and then having to go on a grueling starvation phase is just plain unacceptable for anyone requiring an "optimized state" for day-to-day activities. What if you have to work? Imagine walking around famished to the point of being dizzy. What if you are one of those people who feels nervous, sweaty or uneasy when blood sugar levels starts dropping into the lower regions? What if you have a job where prolonged concentration is demanded? This diet does not work in modern life. People enjoy regularity with meals and depend on it to function. See, it's not just a concern for comfort, but a necessity for proper functioning and development. And in the worst case scenario, it's a matter of survival. I don't know about you, but I don't want my bus driver going on a starvation phase while he/she is responsible for my life or yours. If we were all a bunch of millionaires and had nothing better to do, then giving this crazy dietary practice a swing might seem a little more reasonable. There is yet another reason I don't want you going on this regimen. It was designed for bodybuilders and not for rowers. Imagine trying to row at a high intensity level during a starvation phase. Rowing a test race, for a first place finish, at the end of a starvation phase, when the body is undergoing maximum stress, would be profoundly difficult. Obviously, this does not make sense! This methodology has not been accepted by the bodybuilding community and is certainly not functional for rowing. So what is the catch?

Throughout this training, strong emphasis has been placed on training smarter, over the old brute force methods. If the same old advice is given and followed, -all that can be hoped for is the same old failures. Anyone trying to utilize the ABCDE program throughout the competitive process, would quickly find themselves in a rundown, weary state. In fact, under such repressive conditions, anyone with an ounce of common sense would give up rowing altogether. There is a difference between good stress and masochism. When already at the razors edge, only an insane person would try to engage in repeated bouts of starvation while simultaneously reaching for an intensity level representative of late-stage competitive training. In--stead of constant two week cycles over many months, only ONE overfeeding cycle (without any diet phase) will be employed right be-fore the competition date. How wonderful is this? You get to eat like a pig, without any guilt or adverse health effects. And for those with health concerns, -two weeks worth of overeating will not hurt the body. However, hunger will be an issue when dropping total calories back down to more normal levels. To deal with this, engage in longer endurance training for a period of two weeks or so. Relax, take a break from the rower and do some long power-walks or light jogging; it will make for a nice change of pace and its only two weeks. The longer endurance workouts will create a little nausea, thereby elimin-ating the hunger issue. Just ask any long distance runner, they live this way 24/7.

For most humans, this two week phase will be both a joy and a blessing. For others, -problems getting all the food down will make for an interesting, if not daunting problem. Complaints of not being able to eat due to the previous meal having not yet been fully digested are common. For those experiencing sensitivity in this area, two easy solutions are at hand. First, try eating more dense foods in terms of calories. This way, less can be eaten and volume related problems won't be an issue. You will still want to maintain a good balance of carbs, protein, healthy fats and all the veggies your mother always prescribed. In other words, don't take the idea of "caloric density" to mean triple fudge sundays. Use common sense! Another trick is to stay away from meals containing large amounts of meat. Meat takes a long time to digest and more than any other food, accounts for that "full" feeling. Let's face it, the human body can pass 12 ounces of cottage cheese far faster than 12 ounces of steak. In and out, that's the idea here. Easily digestible alternatives are never hard to find. For most though, moving upward in the "calorie climb" is the easy part and problems are only experienced when reducing calories. Backtracking a little, -there is nothing wrong with eating steak. Some people will have zero problems, regardless of how much food is given. Certain individuals have digestive systems that work like woodchippers. Steak is not the problem here, it is one of sensitivity. Only if encountering such problems, are creative food choices recommended. To give an idea of what overfeeding constitutes, here is an example. Roughly speaking, a 200 pound male eating 2,500 calories a day would then consume a little over 5,000 calories a day for the duration of two weeks. Yeah, it's about twice the normal intake.

There you have it! Only half of the initial program is being borrowed! Once a year for two weeks. Although weight will be gained, that's really not rational behind the overfeeding. It's being done to increase anabolic hormones. During this increase, more aggression will be felt, along with greater strength and endurance. This hormonal surge will produce a noticeable punch and **NO**, this is not psychological trickery! Two weeks of solid hormonal bombardment will allow for full healing and extra energy reserves to boot. Without a doubt, no athlete could ever dream of a better optimized state to compete in. To summarize, you are being given a simple, cost-effective means of shooting hormone levels through the roof, without drugs, cheating, or any other illegal activity/immoral activity. After the race is over, stop shoveling it in.

If you were a marathon runner, this overfeeding phase would not work. For a marathon runner carrying full vertical impact, a huge (negatively speaking) difference would be felt. With rowing, this program works simply because the machine takes most of the brunt from this newly gained weight. A few extra pounds will make no difference when it comes to rowing. Actually, due to the intensity of the competitive training, most competitors will be somewhat underweight. And keep in mind, this newly gained weight is functional weight consisting of more muscle than fat. Adding a few extra pounds will actually prove beneficial and allow for maximal strength recuperation. Don't be surprised if you feel stronger than you have ever felt during this overfeeding cycle.

Chapter 15

Predicting Rowing's Future

At no time in history has bodily perfection achieved such great importance in the public sphere. To exclude any level of ignorance, this focus on perfection has always been visible, but in the media steeped age of today, it has become obsessional. Both sexes, whether young or old, receive daily mental pounding of what perfection should be. Interestingly enough, there has never been a time in history when the general population has fallen to such sedentary lows. Most jobs involve sitting in front of a monitor all day long. Kids sit motionless for hours playing video games and the TV of today is not the TV of old! With the advent of gigantic, ultra-clear, wide-screen displays, it's akin to being at the movie theater; in fact, it's now better than being at the theater. And there is no need to elaborate on the Internet; the problem with obsessional surfing is more than apparent. Add online gaming to the mix and you now have a virtually unlimited grab-bag of sedentary, screen-based activities. For most people, both work and entertainment are primarily comprised of time spent in front of screens. During the early going, the confined and idle nature of this "screen revolution" was somewhat tempered by continuing social activities. Nowadays, social activity is quickly being traded-in for screen time and a lots of it! At no time in history has there been such a need for rowing to be injected into modern society. Some facts have to be accepted; life is not going to change that much in terms of entertainment, work, or for that matter, our newly defined social activities. This "screen obsession" is no fad and anyone hoping for a quick shift back to more traditional activities can dream on; it's going to intensify and enlarge. Even with today's onslaught of technology based items, full market saturation has not been reached. At one time, group exercise, even when light, served as major and highly meaning-ful source of entertainment. As of now and into the distant future, ex-ercise will be relegated as a side activity, -one only engaged in when screen breaks are taken; regardless of opinion, this eventuality is rap-idly taking hold. Modern day exercise has to be simple, fast, effective and must, at all costs, maintain a low complexity profile. Rowing succeeds at all of these demands and fails at not one. An appropriate exercise for a rapidly changing society? Can anyone, from any given standpoint, argue otherwise? Rowing has a very bright future, -one that is undoubtedly due to its modern day appropriateness, on so many levels.

"Rowing is more effective than other forms of exercise!" Many would consider such a statement to be lightly supported, presumptive, if not somewhat conceited; this is not the case! Statements regarding rowing's superiority are exceedingly well grounded. One aspect of great importance, but not often harped on, is how rowing serves as thee preeminent start-up exercise for people at decreased athletic levels. Can anyone expect a sedentary person, who is overweight and out of shape, to go out and start running? Heck, even walking can be a dangerous form of exercise when weight levels are approaching the high end. Discounting weight problems, when exercise is applied by those who are poorly conditioned, there is a high risk of injury. Once again, by virtue of rowing's non-impact, non-weight bearing movement, multi-directional decreases in injuries are achieved and those benefiting the most are the overweight and out of shape. You're not flying through the air, you're not dealing with tremendous impact pressures, you're not twisting into dangerous positions and as a result, injuries such as muscle pulls, fractures, contusions, ankle injuries, acute spinal injuries, neck injuries, ACL tears, along with all other imaginable nightmares, are completely avoided; this is what is meant by "multi-directional." All the while, rowing achieves proper weight levels, proper strength endurance for age/sex, proper metabolic functioning, -all of which lead to increased health, increased psychological functioning, decreased risk of disease and magically enough, decreased injury rates when preforming other physical exercises or activities.

And let us never forget rowing's first name of "INDOOR," nor its importance with regard to avoiding local weather conditions. As trivial as this weather commentary may sound, days lost to inclement conditions sneakily add-up to the point of consuming months per year; under no circumstances can such loses be afforded. As rowing sidesteps the weather problem, its seat position leads to another bonus. Rowing's low-seated position is absolutely perfect for watching TV. Hey, your seated upright and placed at the perfect viewing angle, -might as well take advantage of it.

All in all, rowing has a ton of positive attributes and very few weaknesses. The acknowledgment of these attributes is not put forward in an effort to flaunt rowing's tail feathers, but rather, to illustrate rowing's placement as one of the only beneficial exercises which can be properly grafted into the framework of modern society. A grafting which allows for safety, sustainability and scalability. It's the only exercise gentle enough to get you going and yet, the only one powerful enough to create change to an extent that will guarantee future motivation. Very few exercises allow for such gentleness while at the same time eliciting such a high degree of change in the user. If you have been "sedentary," -as in years worth of screen activity, rowing may in fact be your only option at this point. And luckily, it is the best option!

You might wonder as to what can be expected concerning changes in rowing equipment. This is the beautiful part; rowing machines are not going to change all that much. Most rowing machines from ten years ago still work perfectly and have "looks," along with mechanical functionality, which differ little from today's machines;

nothing much is going to change and the status quo on repairs should not deviate. They might need some occasional tweaking or replacement of foot straps here and there, but that's about all any rower has worry about. In particular, the WaterRower really shines in this area and the other top manufactures aren't too shabby in terms of reliability. Everyone can look forward to minor improvements in noise reduction, strength, beauty and smoothness. These are all welcome changes, but in all honesty, minor in nature. The major changes in the rowing industry are going to come about by way of software developers and happily enough, such changes are already at hand. The main chunk of software has already been developed, but there needs to be more work done in terms of functionality, high polygon count graphics, enhanced networking ability and intuitive graphical user interfaces, reminiscent of what the fine people at Apple Inc., and other various high-end video game designers have put forth.

Being able to row against others in web-based competitions, along with the formation of web-based communities has added a massive amount social networking to a once largely detached rowing community. Rowing's tendency to become an isolated sport, is now a thing of the past; the world has truly become a small place with the advent of online rowing applications. If flesh n' blood humans are not available, hooking up with a training partner from the next town, city, or continent, is no problem at all. You can have a friendly row, or a not so friendly competition; it's entirely up to you. Additionally, voice communications should quickly become standard across all rowing software in the future. The software is quickly evolving and again, working models are already in the wild. However, some of the software is far from perfect at this point. Those not immediately demanding this networking would be wise to give the developers time to get the kinks out and weave in some additional functionality. These technological advances have been a long time coming and serve to eliminate rowing's singular downside, -its isolation!

With competitions such as CRASH-B and BIRC, rowing is here to stay, but what of rowing's shifting popularity. How could anyone trumpet an exercise as the "World's Greatest," when interest in it has waxed and waned for such a long time. By general logic, this would be proof of rowing's non-elite status. Nonsense, many of the world's best exercises have faced diminished interest at one time or another. Take squats as an example.

With regard to weightlifting, squats are now widely regarded as the best exercise for building overall muscle mass. However, the affirmations seen in the present day were not always so forthcoming. Squats fell out of favor for a few decades and at some points, the only athletes engaging in them were Olympic lifters. Only in the last 15 years has squatting regained its past popularity. In the early days of lifting, squats were considered essential to a well rounded physique and no self-righteous lifter would have ever considered going without them. In those days, speaking poorly of the squat was akin to blas-phemy. Even in those early times, with the light of science still largely blacked-out, weightlifting's adherents realized squatting's abil-ity to increase muscle thickness, strength and speed. And it wasn't just the legs receiving benefit, it was the entire body. With little more than some keen "eye-balling" and common sense, these early lifters understood what would take the most gifted sports scientists several more decades to get a grip on. Squats worked and these early lifters knew it. They may not have known exactly how, but knowing the "how" of any given situation is not always important.

And then, in the face of exceedingly positive and what seemed at the time to be incontrovertible evidence, squatting mysteriously died. Many believe squatting lost its popularity due to the pain factor. After all, squatting demands an astonishing level of exertion! Participants have to endure heavy breathing, red-hot burning muscles and nauseated states, often leading to vomiting; regarding the latter, any knowledgeable gym owner will keep a trash can beside the squat rack for this very reason. The initial pain of doing this exercise is rather rough to say the least. Not to mention the tendency to walk a little funny afterward, along with the slightly altered state, coming from the high degree of exertion; and no, it is not a good altered feeling, it is more akin to a "I don't feel quite right," sort of alteration. However, with enough practice, the initial shock subsides and a certain normalcy takes hold; this is true, at least with proper amounts of time being given. No, it will ever be easy, but habituation and adaptation will eventually triumph, giving way to enjoyment of what was once a torturous activity.

In so many ways, rowing is no different and every bit as devious in the early going. As with squats, rowing has put a lot of people in a lot of pain. For the first three minutes or so, rowing seems very easy and suddenly, with no warning whatsoever, the waters get very rough.

With rowing, the work is spread evenly across the entire body. People are not used to this and are generally waiting for some part of their body to fatigue until they are forced to stop. After about 12 minutes into their first row, people are spent and just can't continue. After the next few days of rowing, the fatigue and pain are bad enough to cause permanent cessation. This is the devil's honey; real sweet and simple at first, then things get real sour, -real fast. After a few days of rowing, participants are tired, sore, lacking motivation and start to experience the all too familiar signs of being severely drained. Sooner or later, people have to learn that rowing takes a conditioning phase if they desire continual involvement in the sport. In the end, rowing is still the best exercise, but one differing little from squatting. We don't want rowing to go the way of the "squat" years ago and when initial training begins, ease-in periods should be considered mandatory. With this understanding and hopeful adherence, rowing will have a long and bright future.

As of this day and age, rowing has found itself in a stage of development that can only be described as a "sweet spot." It has undergone increased popularity and has obtained a cult following. Such a popularity level serves as the golden era for any sport; development has not advanced to the point of mass popularity, but unquestionably, strong hooks have been sunk in. As for the people involved, the consistent and cheerful repetition of "love," -almost to the point of veneration, is partly due to rowing's relatively diminutive size and lack of commercialization. There is something to be said for not getting up in the morning and comparing "race times" with Olympic competitors, or highly endorsed athletes. Despite the serious nature of competitions, current ones are more often cast in an easygoing, if not comical atmosphere. If you can't laugh and smile, then what's the point? Generally speaking, no prize money is allotted and this simple lack of monetary reward serves to keep the good "IN," and the bad, "OUT." As a result, there tends to be an almost complete lack of the competitive leeches. Will rowing stay this way and maintain this **low-key by design** approach?

Unless extreme caution is taken, the unfortunate answer is no. All signs are in place for rowing's official "sports status" and legitimization, to go into effect. Throughout the last couple of years, rowers started forming into local clubs and while petite and loosely knit, -the ball has begun rolling. This grouping concept, or that of team identity, is quickly taking hold and serves as the greatest sign of eminent change, in what may be described as a coming polarity shift. Baseball teams originally got started in the e-x-a-c-t same manner; the best guys from each neighborhood would join together and compete against one another and from there, local teams would fuse to represent entire cities. For whatever reason, humans love team sports and their exponential growth throughout the 20th century gives credence to this fact. Once team based competition takes hold, by way of additive solo races or linked machines, it's all over. Teams are then to be had and everybody loves teams. A chilly forecast?

Have no misunderstandings here, the industry is in need of further growth. However, the day when professional rowers come onto the scene and start competing for million dollar contracts, along with other monetary prizes, the beginning of the end will be at hand. Once pristine, -rowing's nature will quickly face pollution by way of greed, corruption and fraud. Does anyone want rowing to mimic cycling in terms of drug use? Some things should never change and rowing's custodians will have to keep a steady gaze on the industry and maintain a certain inflexibility to ensure it doesn't. Once the financiers come in, the fun, ethics and easy going nature of this "cottage industry" will be gone forever. The only permanent solution is to maintain non-monetary competitions.

People have often wondered if this sport would ever make it to the Olympics. As of this date, far more rowers find themselves on land than the water. Rowing's "water-only" Olympic status easily comes into question with such land-based domination; an amusing, if not vexing situation! Most would be amazed to know how many people row on land, but have never so-much as dunked an oar in the water. How does a modern day sport, such as rowing, get into the Olympics? Nowadays, its not so much a matter of petition, but by way of popular force. Do nothing more than become incredibly popular and it's only a matter of time! No better example can be given than snowboarding.

When snowboarding first emerged, participants of this newly formed sport found themselves being loathed by the well ingrained skiing community. Skiers spent more time complaining about snowboarders than anybody could every imagine. However, snowboarding became tremendously popular with the youth. Slope owners, who were eager for the buck, could no longer give attention to the varying complaints. Snowboarding simply generated too much revenue for them to ban it! Contests soon started popping up and a new sport was born. As of this day and age, ask any kid if he/she wants of snowboard, or skies for Christmas? Rest assured, the little tots will be clamoring for the snowboard. Predicting snowboarding's future was easy in this case. After some deliberation, the Olympics had no choice but to let them in. To do otherwise would have designated themselves as a stale competition platform, no longer keeping pace with the modern interests of the day. Will Indoor rowing eventually follow the same route?

As CRASH-B and BIRC have gained large followings, it is only a matter of time. The logistical perfection of this sport, with regard to competition, however scaled, cannot be overlooked. **Specifics are easily outlined:** Climatic conditions are controlled by allowing for indoor or outdoor activity, results are easy to measure, specially groomed tracks/fields/water-systems are unneeded, machines are relatively inexpensive, filming is a breeze (no wild motions, no long distances), competition progress can be shown graphically (any five year old can understand it), Las Vegas bookies will have another sport to bet on (very similar to horse racing), the total package has a low degree of complexity and all competitors use the same machine, which thankfully enough, eliminates material advantages.

All told, this is an Olympic event planer's greatest dream. Generally speaking, Olympic competition is a joy to watch, but a logistical nightmare to pull off. Indoor rowing is an easy fit and will cause little-to-no pain. In fact, adoption is almost guaranteed. However, rowing may get a reprieve and dodge the proverbial bullet for the time being. With the popularity of alternative sports growing at almost exponential levels, -their flair and shock value could easily nudge indoor rowing out of the picture, at least for a while. This would be beneficial for rowing! That is not to imply any evil in Olympic competition, but rather, for consideration to be given to the benefits slower growth and stability.

Chapter 16

Additional Weight Training

It's never really long before the question of whether or not a rower should engage in weight training comes into play. Truth be told, the answer is yes and no: IF ROWING FOR HEATH AND AS-CETICS --**The answer is yes.** IF ROWING FOR COMPETITION --**The answer is absolutely not.**

Lifting in Conjunction with Competitive Rowing

First off, let's get the "No" out of the way. Competitive rowers have been up in arms about this for years. Weight training does not seem to aid rowing times. In fact, weight training hurts competitive rowing times. The intention here is not to start documenting study after study, but rather, to illustrate what many devoted rowers have observed for years. The premise here is very simple; weight training hurts competitive rowing. But, -why?

Muscle fibers adapt to lifting certain weights at certain speeds and their capacity to do so increases with repeated practice. With rowing, you are lifting (horizontally) a certain percentage of your body weight plus the erg's resistance at any given setting. Your speed and corresponding number of reps also factor into the equation. With weightlifting, you are doing the same thing, but in a far different manner. The problem here lies with the differences in weight and the number of repetitions. Weightlifting almost always relies on lower reps and higher weights. Rowing on the other hand, uses far less weight, with higher reps and to a greater degree, stresses slow twitch muscle fibers. We now have a big problem on our hands. By weight-lifting, the body is conditioned away from optimal rowing perform-ance and geared towards other activities, such as football.

Factor in the other end of the spectrum, -with long distance run-ning serving as an example. In this case, rowing is more intense and its total duration is shorter. With rowing being more intense than long distance running and less intense than weightlifting, it must be assumed that rowing occupies some middle ground. Rowing has been referred to as a strength endurance exercise, -right? So which is it closer to, STRENTH or ENDURANCE, or is just some oddball sit-ting perfectly on the fence? Generally speaking, rowing utilizes an 80/20 muscle fiber ratio. That's 80% activation of slow twitch muscle fibers and 20% activation for fast twitch muscle fibers. There is the answer: Rowing is primarily an endurance based sport. Fast-twitch fibers are activated, but 20% is hardly substantial as far a hard-core activation goes. During sprinting (500-1,000 meters), the fast twitch value of 20% would be expected to drastically increase, but don't be so fast to judge! This number may not increase as much as expected. Remember, the rowing movement is long (compound) and even though a tremendous amount of work is being done while sprinting, it is still not a rapid movement in comparison to the muscular contraction rates of other physical activities. Compare how many times a track athlete's quadriceps will contract (at full sprinting speed) for a three second period. Now, compare this to the firing rate of a rower's quadriceps at full sprinting speed for the same three second time period. There is a big difference here! The rowers are not even close. Rowing, even when on the fast side, is not about heavy loads, or quick muscular contractions. Rowing is a slow firing, strength endurance exercise and must be trained for as such. Train too far under, such as long distance running, or too far over, such as weight training and the body is conditioned away from what creates optimal performance. Yet another problem exist with the movement itself.

Most weightlifting exercises, such seated rowing (don't confuse with indoor rowing), are not compound exercises. Compound exercises are dependent upon coordination! This coordination is exceedingly importance and should never be discounted. The best example to illustrate the importance of proper coordination is the billiards analogy. Breaking power in billiards is not simply a function of strength alone. By most standards, I am a fairly strong man, but for much of my life, nothing more than a weak break was to be had on the pool table. It would not be until years of practice that I was able to break the balls with a professional level of power. Well, -what exactly changed? I learned to coordinate my various muscles in a correct time-linked fashion in order to create power. It's all about the timing of one muscle firing right after another in what might be referred to as a proper time-linked sequence. This is why some very small women can break billiard balls harder than many men who are two and three times their size! The exact same principle works with throwing a bowling ball. Again, I have seen women who are half my size generate far more power. They too, through years of practice, have developed good muscular coordination! Not only are they more powerful, but far cleaner in the movement. As with billiards and bowling, this proper muscle linking is critical in rowing and it's especially important during competition. While total explosive power is of little concern with rowing, enhanced coordination makes individual strokes more powerful, with less effort. Rowing's unique compound movement cannot be duplicated with weights.

Certain arguments for weightlifting while rowing could be made on the basis of expected increases in GH resulting from hyper-intense large muscle stimulation (squatting, bench, seated-rows). It goes without saying that GH has positive effects on just about everything dealing with exercise performance and yes, this goes for both endurance and sprinting exercises. GH seems to have proven itself as thee all-encompassing wonder juice and has recently been cast as the fountain of youth. However, the type of muscle conditioning brought about by exercises such as squatting, does not jive with rowing. This we already know! But, one could make the assertion of increased GH levels offsetting wrongfully (directionally speaking) trained musculature (resulting from weightlifting) which now has to be employed in rowing. In other words, they have poorly developed musculature for mid-range (strength endurance) specific exercises, but great physical health, which may, -at least by their logic, increase athletic performance, thereby making up for such incidental negatives. I'm not even close to being comfortable with such an assertion! In this case, the stopwatch is the only real judge. The health benefits of lifting, while of great benefit, do NOT enhance racing performance over "rower only" training and there is no getting around this fact.

It is really not much of a surprise as to why so many competitive rowers have turned to weightlifting for an edge; In retrospect, football players, hockey players, basketball players and baseball players all lift weights. These sports all utilize quick explosive movements and there is a need for extra meat padding. Most figure it works for other sports and as logic would follow, it must work for rowing. IT DOES NOT WORK FOR ROWING! For those pursuing competition, -stay away from the weights; it's just too counterproductive.

Lifting in Conjunction with Non-competitive Rowing

Lifting in conjunction with non-competitive rowing is a match made in heaven. In this situation, we do not care if weightlifting slightly alters rowing performance in a negative manner. Desired goals can still be easily reached, whether it be fitness or fat loss.

Negative effects from non-specific muscular conditioning do not exist outside the competitive sphere. In this case, we are striving for a balanced, healthy body and not winning the gold.

One thing which has to be cleared up is the concept of cross-training. Adding weightlifting to any rowing regimen is not cross-training, -at least not by my standards! Cross-training, by proper definition, consists of doing other cardio exercises via some other sport or activity. This is not what is going on here. Additionally, modern weightlifting is done in very intense, brief workouts. That's right, no more than 20 minutes. Actually, the real time limit is closer to 12-15 minutes. Almost all research is pointing to the most efficient muscle building programs being fast, intense and infrequent. Strap in, burn the muscles out and the workout is done! Anything else is just counterproductive. So, when is the best time to start? If desired, weightlifting can be introduced once adequate weight loss has been achieved, along with a descent fitness level. Two basic ideas support this notion.

First, weightlifting intensely stimulates the hunger mechanism. Aerobic exercise does the exact opposite and even instills mild nausea. After lifting, many people will gorge themselves to pacify this intense hunger. How many fat muscle-bound guys have you seen in your life? I've seen tons. How many fat endurance athletes have you seen in your life? Such occurrences are rare! The point being, you will want to get your weight under control before adding weightlifting to the mix. Additionally, new evidence points to lean bodies burning calories in a more efficient manner. In other words, you'll want to get lean in order to maintain this "leanness." This should all be done before the lifting starts. People with higher body fat levels not only have to put up with the extra weight, but also the added insult of inefficient fat burning. Talk about pouring salt in the wound.

The second reason is understandable, but oftentimes overlooked; a body in good shape will show an increased adaptive response to weightlifting. The reasons behind this are as numerous as they are obvious. Increased heart, lung and circulatory function will add up to a lot in terms of how the body responds to lifting weights. Less obvious factors such as improved liver function, count for more than most would think. Excess fat puts a great stain on liver due to increased estrogen and excessive estrogen is a big no-no when it comes to lifting. The list goes on and on and on, but there is no need to go over each and every heath metric of "leanness" and its corresponding benefits; this is commonly understood. Please don't ignore this advice! Get lean and then lift! If you're already lean, then be my guest and unite the two.

With the question of "when to start" out of the way, choosing a specific type of lifting still remains. Truth be told, its a personal decision. Hard-core powerlifting, bodybuilding, or high-rep lifting with lower weights are all available. All three are perfectly good choices in terms of health benefits. However, most will want to leave out the high-rep lifting regimens. These high repetition routines are typically done to give that super lean/vascular/ripped look with minimal bulk. Trust me, -rowing will do more than enough to keep the ripped-and-tight appearance more than dominant. When stacking rowing with weightlifting, obtaining that sought after vascular look will be of little concern. Always remember, the stacking of these exercises is not additive, it's synergistic. For most, the question will be between powerlifting and bodybuilding. Again, the choice is yours. Some will want to go with powerlifting simply for its strength enabling properties, while others will choose general bodybuilding for its ascetic advantages. Bodybuilding has one advantage over powerlifting in that it is far safer and it doesn't take a genius to understand the visual effects.

At this point, we have to be honest with ourselves. In this day and age, much of the interest in lifting weights lies in the ascetics. Sure, its also being done for the health benefits, but if little more than health were given, would such popularity remain. I'm not about to get into any arguments concerning the matter! Let me put it this way, I'm just happy people are lifting, even if it's for exceedingly vain purposes. Taking pride in one's appearance is not as sinful as some people may suggest. That being said, most bodybuilding routines utilize three sets of 10-12 reps per exercise and this is how you will want to go about it. Lifting gives a beautiful symmetrical appearance and a little extra strength never hurt anyone. Rowing only has one weak spot and that's the chest. While the back muscles are fully activated, the chest is only utilized in an indirect fashion. A little "evening out" in this area is highly recommended for most rowers.

As for general advice when it comes to weight training, -well, this is yet another topic which is far beyond the scope of this book. If you are not well schooled in this area, there are plenty of experts out there who are more than willing to help out. Most bodybuilders are so obsessed with their chosen sport that they will talk, talk, talk and then talk for a couple more hours about everything from routines to Met-Rx shakes. There are only a handful of rowing experts on this planet, but seemingly endless supplies of bodybuilding experts willing to put forth every tip, technique, theory and story.

Only common sense can be offered. Bodybuilding takes time, so don't overdo it. This whole blood-and-guts approach to lifting is something perpetrated by foolish individuals using bucket-loads of drugs. Follow their methodologies and you'll end up in an ER room with severe muscle/tendon damage. For those not having viewed the aftermath of full pectoral tear, it is not a pretty sight. Weightlifting is more about patience and playing it smart than it is about being an aggressive maniac. Lifting extremely hard in initial phases only results in massive soreness and it is this "soreness" which makes beginners quit. In other words, it's no different from rowing, so take your time. Also, be sure to increase max lifting poundages in small increments and don't increase to any given weight without first being able to do at least seven clean reps with a weight five pounds lighter. This simple rule will keep you from experiencing a great deal of agony. One last thing, - please check your ego at the door.

Chapter 17

Questions, Arguments, Answers

Q: Could you please explain the damper setting on the Concept2

A: Sure can. Concept2 machines come with a funny little dial on the side. This is the damper setting and this little lever has single-handedly become the greatest point of confusion for the entire industry. Many people have attempted to explain its function, -some with great success and others, ...well, we won't talk about that. Even for those with a good understanding of the damper, -finding the correct words for explaining it has been difficult at times. One of the key areas of confusion results from interplay between the damper setting and the actual speed of rowing. This gets tricky due to more than one factor being involved. However, the main issue in need of explanation is why any given athlete would choose one setting over another; past coverage of this topic has been given by many parties, but more often than not, its been a bit lean. This is clearly a case when semantics are of great importance, with very detailed explanations being in need.

The Concept2 website gives a good start at understanding the damper and puts forth two basic premises. First, no matter what setting has been selected, -the faster the rowing pace, the more effort there will be required. After all, blades are being spun against the air (which serves as resistance) and if the fan is to move faster, more applied energy is needed. This dispels one myth which revolves around increases in intensity being solely dependent up increasing the damper setting. Concept2 then goes on to comment on the damper settings and gives the analogy of bicycle gearing. This provides for a good start, but a little more in the way of elaboration is in need.

The explanation given by Concept2, concerning the damper setting working in a similar fashion to bicycle gearing, does provide for an exceedingly good analogy. The best way to understand gearing differences is to watch Tour de France riders going up hills. Some are pedaling very fast with lighter loads, while others are pedaling slower, with greater loads. It is obvious they are are using different gearing, but why would a bunch of men, having similar builds, with almost cloned-like physical characteristics, show such sharp contrast in gearing choice. After all, they are all roughly the same weight, riding the same distances and utilizing the same courses under the same conditions. This makes no sense at all. If the biking world were filled with athletes having different physiques (which it is not), a logical person would expect a more athletically built person to utilize higher gearing, while a slimmer, smaller competitor, with greater endurance qualities, to prefer lower gearing. This would, after all, make complete sense. But let's not get too far ahead of ourselves with such questions. Focus needs to be given to the question at hand. Why do certain bike riders use certain gearing and why is the difference between them so darn large!

Choosing any given gear depends on server factors. Metrics dealing with muscle fiber ratios, cardiovascular conditioning (VO2 max) and the body's ability to deal with lactic acid all factor in, but one factor, more than any other, seems to be the scientists' choice as most influential. Generally speaking, those who have a high biochemical aptitude for dealing with lactic acid, tend to thrive at lower gearing. Having a high percentage of slow-twitch muscle fibers, along with a high VO2 Max, also plucks the strings of importance, but in this case, such factors are "assumed" due to an extraordinary ability to manage lactic acid. Conversely, there are athletes who have high VO2 max levels, along with a large percentage of slow-twitch muscle fibers and still do not have an incredible ability to manage lactic acid. Having an extraordinarily high lactic acid threshold is a genetically determined trait and a very rare gift. Training can lead to dramatic improvements in an athlete's lactic acid threshold, but entering into the elite category can only be attributed to mommy and daddy's DNA. And there you have the final piece of the puzzle as to why certain people find it easier to utilize lower gearing than others. Lower gearing has the wonderful attribute of placing the muscles under less contractual strain, whereby faster recovery can be achieved. However, this advantage cannot be utilized by everyone because low gearing is heavily aerobic, lending itself to high lactic acid levels. This increase in lactic acid decreases performance, U-N-L-E-S-S the body has a rare genetic gift to biochemically nullify it. Hello Lance Armstrong!

Historically, not all cyclists favored low gearing and this was true for many of its greats. Somewhat surprisingly, they too, along with low gearing cyclists, had exceedingly high VO2 max levels. One thing is known for sure, VO2 max levels are in no way a determining factor when it comes to the selection of low versus high gearing. Do some of these athletes prefer high gearing specifically because they have more general strength and lack the lactic acid advantage? The obvious answer seems to be yes. Given the complexity of the topic, an entire book could be dedicated, but for general understanding, this will suffice. What any given rower needs to know is that individual damper settings are extremely variable. Most people prefer a setting somewhere in the middle. That is not altogether surprising, but at the same time, sticking the damper dial in the middle may not be best for you. With the Concept2, experimenting with different damper settings must take place. You may have very unique genetics making for extraordinary performances at either the high, or low end. As a side note, those engaging in shorter races, at faster paces, generally prefer slightly higher gearing. Doing otherwise would set up a situation where too many reps would be required and a stroke rate, -far too fast for comfort; the entire body would be violently contracted and expanded like an accordion. Due to the short distance and accordion like movement of rowing, higher gearing allows for not only greater comfort, but greater efficiency. The distance and kinetic nature create a limiting factor in this case. As for longer races, -decisions must be made. Once competition is at hand, please start experimenting!

Q: Can anything be done to stop back soreness from rowing?

A: This is normal for many people and I have experienced this a few times myself. These experiences generally come on after a long layoff. After a couple of weeks, these muscle aches vanish completely. If you are experiencing such pain, back off and take up a more gentle training regimen. Rowing, although painful on the back at first, is actually good for the back and serves to strengthen it. Many doctors actually recommend rowing as a cure for chronic back soreness.

**please note, if you have had previous back injuries or suspect something is seriously wrong, please see a doctor.

Q: I've done very well at indoor rowing and I'm planning to start rowing on the water. Are there any real differences between the two?

A: Yes, static (indoor rowing) and dynamic (on the water) rowing are very different. There are two major differences here. When rowing in a boat, the oar sweeps out on an arc motion. During this arc, you are only applying maximum force during the middle of the stroke. This is when the oar face is at a 90 degree angle (to the boat) and positioned maximally for water movement. Rowing machines work in a completely different manner; maximum power can be applied throughout the motion. This simple fact completely changes the feel between the two.

Also, when rowing on an indoor machine, the person rowing has to put forth more energy to decelerate his or her body. While rowing on the water, things change a bit to the rower's advantage. The rower's forward body movement (when coming to the catch) is dampened due to the forward movement of the boat and by consequence, the person rowing has less of a need to control the deceleration of their body.

Lastly, when rowing on the water, you're usually not alone. You have to stay in good timing with the other rowers. This is not as easy as it looks and takes time to learn! You can have the best erg times in the world and still yet, be horrid on the water. Rowing on the water looks fairly simply, but it's not!

Q: Sometimes my legs tire out and I use my arms a little more to give the legs a couple seconds of rest. Is this bad.

A: The answer is no; after all, you may not have a choice. What you are doing is called cheating the ratio. People rarely comment on the rower's ability to control the percentage of upper body vs. lower body muscle usage to complete each stroke. If the lower body tires, the arms can be engaged earlier, with a more intense heave given. This alone will take much of the stress off the legs and gives a few seconds of needed rest, -just as your doing. On the flip side, if your arms are burning out, you can just use more of your legs by engaging the arms later in the rowing movement, with less of a heave. Every rower knows about this, but most never talk about it. Abnormal top/bottom usage ratios are generally the result of poor body management and for that reason, most rowers will never admit to it. However, if you're unbalanced, or in pinch while rowing, a little cheating of the ratio can be done and everybody does it to some extent. Keep in mind, the idea is not to cheat, but to keep the correct balance. Cheating this way should only be done when absolutely needed and not relied upon as a strategy. It is no different than watching a rock climber who hangs from one arm (straightened) for a couple of seconds. Although appearing to be nothing more than an exceedingly brave act, this is in fact a resting position. While fascinating to watch, rock climbers have little desire to utilize this technique, but at times, they have little other choice; the same goes for rowing.

Q: Is aerobic exercise really needed? I know many people who only lift weights and are doing just fine.

A: Cardio training is an absolute "essential" in today's society. I don't care who you are, -it must be undertaken. If a healthy body is desired, it cannot be avoided. Cardio training is much more than just strengthening the lungs. It strengthens the entire vascular system, muscles and serves to alter the biochemical functioning of the body. There is a reason why experienced rowers and cyclists can maintain high heart rate levels without a problem and football players, after an entire winter of laziness, drop dead on the first 85 degree day. Such conditioning produces a protective effect.

As is well known, cardio training dramatically lowers the risk of multiple of diseases, but when taken out of context, nothing impressive can be said of this preventive effect; after all, lots of health boosters do in fact decrease certain diseases here and there. The amazing part revolves around the specific diseases which cardio tends to eliminate and those just happen to be the ones which kill us most of the time. To go on to list them all would be a waste of time, as most people are all too aware of them. I too have known certain people who hate cardio and refuse to do it. Conversely, there are many people who love cardio and would not consider going a day without it. Whatever your stance, if you're not doing it, your seriously putting your health at risk. —End of story.

Q: I have read articles on high intensity exercise and they keep mentioning something called IGF-1. What is this "IGF-1" thing.

A: Insulin Growth Factor-1 (IGF-1) is produced from GH. It serves as the premier activator of the AKT signaling pathway, which by short definition, is the light-switch for cellular growth. Almost all of the anabolic benefits from GH are really coming from IGF-1. When people in the sports science world speak of GH benefits, -what they are actually referring to is IGF-1. Due to the parental relationship, making references to GH is perfectly fine.

Q: I'm a large rower and currently dominating in my erg times. I'm going to start racing on the water soon, but was told that my heavy body would place more downward pressure on the hull and would hurt my times.

A: It is true, a heavier body will place more downward pressure on the hull and create more drag. However, the benefit of having a more powerful body will offset the added resistance coming from the hull sinking. One overrides the other. Don't worry about it.

Q: Is rowing a good exercise for an older adult like myself?

A: Yes, indoor rowing is perfect for a number of reasons. Older adults are always seen using pools for physical therapy. Light swimming is obviously beneficial and touts itself as one of the few zero impact exercises out there. Pools are great, but hard to come by. Not to mention, not everyone enjoys them. Trust me, many older adults would rather skip the bathing suits altogether and stick with the indoor rower. Getting wet is enjoyable when your young and in good shape. Other than that, it's a drag.

Older adults often suffer from horrid rounding of the spine. Because rowing uses the back muscles to such a large extent, this rounding tendency is counteracted. There is no valid reason for so many older adults to be in this condition! I have seen older adults (over the age of 75) who row daily and have no spinal degeneration or rounding problems whatsoever. With every rowing stroke, you are curling the spine forward at the catch and then bending the spine backward at the end of the drive. This repeated motion keeps the back healthy, supple and acts to counteract the fixed rigidity that accompanies old age. However, rowing's gentleness and the lack of joint pounding are probably the main advantages for older adults. Older adults cannot engage in impact-centric exercises! Lastly, need I mention older adults enjoying the "rocking chair effect" of rowing? Ok, forget the joke, it was a bad one! In all seriousness, if an older adult gets into rowing, they may never get into the rocking chair, or the wheelchair for that matter.

Q: If you could only buy only one rowing machine, which would be chosen?

A: I enjoy both the Concept2 and the WaterRower. These machines are very different, but both are of the utmost quality. For the good of the consumer, there should never be a single manufacturer. There is room in the rowing industry for two great companies and I have no desire to take sides. Both companies have EARNED their reputations as producers of "A" level rowing machines. I have not chosen these two products for review, you have! Ask rowers which machines they prefer and time and time again, you will hear WaterRower and Concept2 being mentioned more than any other.

Q: Do you value competition when it comes to rowing?

A: At my age, absolutely not, but many people love the process, sense of achievement and the community aspect brought about by competition. Personally, I view competitions as a way to promote rowing and as a way for companies to lock in a "network effect" for their rowing machines. There is NO evil in the latter. As for competitors, the competitive process should serve as more than just competition. When approached correctly, competition should act as an aid for ushering in a life-long commitment to health. Ultimately, that is what it's about. Having a body which functions as it should, for as long as it should.

Q: What is your take on Concept2 slides?

A: The Concept2 slides were designed to create a more realistic rowing simulation. One downside of slide usage, revolves around the athlete, once moving back-and-forth, now remaining roughly stationary. You may remember earlier material, thoroughly detailing rowing's sense of movement, as being the main reason for rowing's enjoyment factor. Without such movement, this book would not have been written. Indoor rowing is now its OWN sport and attempts at perfect water simulation are of little benefit for people who never intend to compete on the water. However, slides serve as good way to link machines together. I'm extremely happy with Concept2's decision to keep the slides as an optional add-on and not pushing them on the consumer. A very good decision on the part of Concept2. This way, everyone is happy.

Q: I was told that rowing machines with "stationary" heads, such as the Concept2 (Without the slides) and WaterRower, create more load stress at the catch and by consequence, "may" create more injuries.

A: Yes, I have heard such rumblings and its not coming from the people at Concept2 or WaterRower. The fixed-head designs of the Concept2 (without the slides) and the WaterRower both have excellent safety records. I do not believe the load-stress levels of fixed-head rowing machines to be at levels warranting even remote concern. These machines have had over two decades worth of safety assurance. The designs are non-impact, non-weight bearing and obviously benefit from tandem leg usage, which works to further distribute the force. And still yet, certain individuals speak of these machines as possibly causing injury. What injuries are they speaking of? You can get injured doing anything (rowing is certainly no exception), but these machines have maintained the highest levels of safety imaginable. If you don't believe me, take a look at the data for yourself. You might be surprised to find very little information on the subject. Why you ask? This is because only injuries are tracked and if injuries are extremely rare or of little consequence, tracking is forsaken. Compare this to other sports and quickly enough, stark differences will be seen. When is the last time you heard of an indoor rower tearing an ACL. When is the last time you heard indoor rowers suffering muscle tears, fractures, or severe sprains. Sure, people do complain of back soreness from time-to-time, but is "this" back soreness an injury? Sore muscles, typically resulting from poor conditioning, do not in any way equate to INJURY and certainly not spinal injuries! Brutishly awakening sluggish musculature, especially after exceedingly long naps, brings forth painful reprisals; this should be of no surprise. The musculature will be more than just a bit cranky! That being said, a healthy person should easily be able to handle the loads of fixed-head machines. Again, such attempts at reinventing the wheel and putting forth false danger flags, along with further calls for "safety-revamping," are totally and completely unwarranted.

Any given person could come out tomorrow and invent a steering wheel that would be easier to turn than the modern power-assisted versions on the market today. Would it be accurate to say these new wheels decrease injury. Absolutely not, very few people are injured by the turning mechanism in modern steering wheels. There is no need to lessen the load-stress in this case! The same goes for high-end, fixed-head rowing machines. No rowing machine is perfect, but this painful rhetoric of company X and Y having machines that are rightfully regarded as an extremely safe pieces of exercise equipment, while company Z touts their revamped machine, designed for greater simulation, as being the theoretically safer, thereby eliminating some undetermined, immeasurable, phantom risk of injury, -is somewhat misleading.

Q: Will you review any other rowing machines in the future.

A: Again, this is up to you the consumer. If another machine comes along that wins the hearts and minds of the general public, along with seeing heavy adoption, then it will be reviewed. This is your choice, not mine. Make no mistake, I am not the gatekeeper of rowing reviews, it is you! The only requirement on my end is for machines to allow for the sense of motion (fixed head). Options against this are fine, as long as they are options. Again, Concept2 slides serve as a good example.

Q. Is there any specific body type which is best for rowing?

A: Yes, there actually is. Successful rowers tend to be tall, have high sitting heights, long arms and are generally more "muscled" than other endurance athletes at similar body fat levels. This is true of successful men and women in the sport. Don't worry if you don't match the criteria, most rowers don't. Every sport has a black sheep which totally dominates in spite of not having the prerequisite build. Think Janet Evans, -with nothing more than a slim, petite build, she dominated the world of swimming. She was amazing!

Q: I'm what many consider to be an accomplished athlete and competitive rowing has sparked my interest. My father was also an incredible athlete and still is. With good genetics, what time frame should be expected to become a good rower and from there, to win, or at least place favorably in competitions?

A: This is an interesting question. Assuming you have a good distribution of slow twitch muscle fibers, it should take about three years to really peak. Why would it take a grade "A" athlete this long you ask? It takes time for the body to teach itself to become powerful and efficient in any movement. It is as much about training the motor pathways as it is about strengthening the heart, lungs and muscles.

On the flip side, if you are an athlete with a high percentage of fast twitch muscle fibers, you are going to have some trouble. The good news? -Well, your body can adapt to these situations to some extent. For many decades, scientists believed fast and slow twitch muscle fiber ratios to be genetically locked. Recently, this belief has proven false. Muscle fiber distribution can be shifted through specific training. Now granted, don't expect a huge change, but a slight shifting of a few percentage points over a couple of years time can be expected. This revelation, however promising, may not be enough for those who are geared too much in the fast twitch direction. Again, if you are an athlete with an extremely high percentage of fast twitch muscle fibers, I would recommend finding a different sport to compete in. You will never make it in longer duration races and there is really no point in doing races under 2,000 meters. Baring some miracle, you will most likely spend a lot of time being upset and hopelessly trying to compete with people who are out of your league. Keep in mind, rowing for health can be done and when it comes to that, muscle fiber ratios are of little concern. This topic has only been highlighted due to its importance with the standard 2,000 meter races.

Q: I read an article explaining that exercising at a faster pace only burns slightly more calories than at a slower pace and by keeping a slower pace, longer durations could be obtained, along with more calories being burned. As a result, I was instructed to just engage in longer duration exercises at very slow pacing. Do you agree with this?

A: No, the writer you were referring to probably didn't consider the effects of full out sprinting, or the highly intense pacing seen in competitive training. This author was probably referring to slightly increased intensity. This is not the same as the sprinting done during the HIIT program! We have concrete evidence of the superiority of HIIT vs. the longer endurance based routines. The same goes for competitors training for 2,000 races. Use common sense, -how many of these people have problems with obesity? These 2,000 meter races only take a few minutes to finish, but the results are outstanding. Perhaps not as good as HIIT (when done correctly), but still, the results are amazing. The fat-loss effects regarding the 2,000 meter races are little spoken of due to racing's focus being on competition, but the effects are still there. The only need for longer durations, with less intensity, would be in cases involving cardiac concerns, or other health issues demanding limited intensity.

Q: I'm currently obese (312 lbs, at 5' 9") and was looking to start losing some weight. I picked rowing specifically because of the lack of joint pounding. Could you recommend a rowing machine and workout program.

A: Rowing is fine for people who are overweight, but not for the massively obese. If you were to row at this weight, you would be risking herniation. The rowing movement involves pulling the legs up the abdomen/chest and under such circumstances, a high degree of abdominal distention could be dangerous. I would ONLY recommend swimming as a safe exercise while at such high weight levels.

Nothing else is safe during such circumstances. Figure out a way to get access to a pool and get-on with it. When coming within 80 pounds of your target weight for a man of your height and age, -then, and only then, can rowing be undertaken. Take is slow!

Q: Don't you think your being overly protective when you advise people to stay away from almost all other sports except rowing?

A: No, it's a tactical decision. It's unfortunate, but a great number of modern sports are dangerous. Engage in them for a long enough period of time and damage will be incurred; it is a rock solid guarantee. And yes, some of this damage will last a lifetime! The problem at hand mushrooms to gigantic proportion when considering modern day life expectancies. At the end of the 19th century, the average European man or women was lucky if he or she made it to 40. As of this day and age, many developed countries are edging well over 80 year life spans. It is almost as if general logic has not caught up with modern day life expectancies. When finding yourself crippled by age 40, the "situation" may have to be dealt with for another 40 years or more. Not being able to function WHEN and WHERE needed, will prove to be far more oppressive than most could ever imagine. Animating such logic by way of gory medical examples is unnecessary. I'm just asking people to use their heads, do the math and not be one of "those" people. It is a choice.

Q: A sports scientist recently claimed that activities such as swimming and rowing were inferior (at burning calories) to that of weight bearing exercises such as running. I was told to stop wasting my time and just take up running.

A: Here we go again! These sorts of comments keep coming up and fending them off is getting a bit tiresome, but I'll give this one a go. Activities such as swimming and rowing are loved because of their great ability to massively reduce injuries and I hope we can all agree on this single point. As for the burning of calories, his or her logic is a little off center. Well, in actuality, such an assertion would be accurate for those casual swimming laps in a pool. I didn't know if anyone had noticed, but swimming pools in no way stop anyone from engaging in intense or fast paces. These experts act as if there are signs above pools saying, "DANGER: NO INTENSE OR FAST SWIMMING ALLOWED." The same thing goes for rowing! You can row as fast as needed and rowing machines are designed to give even the greatest athletes an unreachable ceiling.

Watch top rowers competing in the 2,000 meter races and in just a few minutes time, they will look as though death is upon them. If you don't believe me, buy a Concept2 machine and try to break the world record for 2,000 meters. After you're done, please feel free to call me after the paramedics have taken the oxygen mask off your face and I'll be happy to listen to any comments you have regarding the reduced intensity of this inferior, non-weight bearing exercise called rowing. With any luck, the hypoxic stupor will have worn off long before the mistake is made. Again, look at competitive swimmers and you'll see the same situation taking place. Have you ever seen the intensity level of the butterfly stroke? Do competitive swimmers look as though they have body fat problems? Do top rowers?

Obviously, the same old arguments keep being made for the same old reasons. Some of these assertions are little more than wrongfully biased opinions, while others are nothing more than erroneous logic. In the case of logical errors, most are due to old chart information. Certain "calories burned" per exercise charts are antiquated and contain grossly misleading data. Newer and more accurate charts list additional columns for "increased intensity" for any specific exercise. And the differences (calories burned) in the "increased intensity" columns are shocking when compared to the "low" and "moderate" columns. Obviously, not everyone is looking at these newer charts. Not to mention, their definition (even in the newer charts) of intense and YOUR definition of intense may not be the same. In other words, the fat burning effects of the HIIT routine may be far greater than what is claimed even in the "intense" column.

Q: You talked about bodybuilding adding too much muscle and related health concerns. Later on, you advocate lifting weights. Isn't this a contradiction.

A: Extra muscle is good, but extreme bulk is not. Obtaining the muscular level of an Olympic gymnast (or even slightly above) is about perfect, -at least in my estimation. They have functional muscle, great ascetics, but are in no way overdeveloped. Bigger and more developed than your average human? Sure they are, but that's not a problem. The problems begin when people start obtaining the same level of muscularity as the incredible hulk.

Q: I spoke with a few fitness experts about cross-training and they told me that cross-training was in fact valid. You seem to disagree with them. What gives?

A: This is actually somewhat of a complicated topic and every effort will be made for clarification. As mentioned earlier, cross-training does work on paper and the "mathematics" regarding the potential for caloric burning are in fact valid. Still yet, problems exist and these problems are NOT surmountable.

Let's take a very hypothetical example. If you were to ride up a hill with Greg LeMond (in his prime), you would burn more calories than he would even though you were staying right with him. Greg's muscles have been conditioned for the exercise and are extremely efficient at NOT wasting needed energy reserves (calories). Greg's highly coordinated sport-specific conditioning results in almost perfect economy of movement which impedes extraneous and/or poorly timed firing of muscles. For Greg, the net result is less calories being burned than that of a rookie. This is good for the rookie and seems to prove the whole cross-training theory. The next day, you may want to go out and do some stair-climbing or whatever else is unfamiliar and keep repeating this cycle of doing varied exercises to which the body is not accustomed. All the while, you're burning more calories than the actual people, who are singular, day-to-day practitioners of such sports or activities. It all sounds great on paper, but there are some serious problems with this theory.

In order to climb the hill with Greg, you would have to be in very good shape. Unfortunately, this is not the case for most people. Most people would have to quit after a few minutes and by doing so, any assumed benefits are canceled-out. Cross-training implies that athletes are already in extremely good condition and in all cases, success is based on keeping pace with the highly trained athletes for any given activity. If an athlete were already in good condition, or at least in good enough condition to keep up with Greg, why would they need cross-training in the first place; this is illogical thought. In most cases, only a fraction of the given "exercise time" is completed and the benefits of higher caloric burning (for untrained athletes) serve no purpose. If I were to go out and play soccer tomorrow, I would burn far more calories than a regular player. Unfortunately, I would be completely dead in the water after five minutes and would not receive any of the benefits that a regular player would after playing one hour. It's kind of obvious, even though I burned more calories for the first five minutes and would theoretically continue to do so, it's of little value if I can't keep going the distance. This is foolishness!

The larger problem is one of soreness. We have all been sore after doing unfamiliar exercises and unfortunately, cross-training relies on unfamiliar exercises by its very definition. This soreness will stop you in your tracks! Let's face it, who among us is willing to walk around in constant pain all of the time. Pain is something which all of us have to deal with from time to time, but most humans are not mentally strong enough to handle it in a non-stop fashion.

Lastly, two other ideas were presented. One revolved around the cross-training advantage being overvalued. Bike riders do not cross-train! World class runners do not cross-train! Their body fat levels are extremely low without cross-training. In fact, it is almost impossible to achieve lower body fat levels and remain healthy. All of these athletes, in separate disciplines, have obtained near perfect body fat levels and no cross-training has taken place!

The other idea revolved around people wanting one exercise to solely concentrate on and maintain as a hobby. It's part of their identity and that's the way people like it. Such a rational may seem trivial, but it's truly important. People have a strong desire to master one and only one activity. Who wants to ride a bike one day, go stair climbing the next and then finalize the week by sprinting on a high school track field. This is silly and almost nobody enjoys it. When is the last time you talked to a superbly conditioned athlete who defined themselves as a cross-trainer? I hope this long explanation clears things up.

Q: What is the most misunderstood concept in rowing?

A: There is no major concept which is highly misunderstood, save the damper, which is nothing more than a physics problem (a complicated one when factoring in body chemistry), but there is a secondary issue that can be elaborated on. What has been spoken of throughout this work is how rowing is a unique strength endurance exercise, allowing for a massive amount of work to be done in a very short period of time, while still maintaining itself as an aerobic exercise. What isn't always understood is how exactly this is accomplished, THAT IS, -with rowing maintaining itself as a highly aerobic exercise. Because of rowing's long compound movement (easily exceeding most other sports), when the exercise is sped up, it remains an aerobic exercise because of the long compound distance creating a situation whereby exceedingly fast muscular contraction rates are all but impossible. This is a secret which allows rowing it to maintain itself as an aerobic exercise while at faster pacing. Having the seat take much of the weight is an obviously factor, but the exceedingly long movement also plays an important role. Very few people understand, or even give consideration to this very unique aspect of rowing.

Q: Indications were made for the chest being in need of more direct work due to this being a weak spot of rowing. I have seen both static charts and animated movies directly showing the chest being utilized in rowing.

A: The chest is worked to the extent of having to bring the arms forward during the recovery, but this is only the weight of the arms! The chest muscle is not utilized to any great degree in rowing! These so-called kinetic experts are completely wrong. It will be 100 years from now and let me assure you, people will still be confused between what the back muscles do and what the chest muscles do.

Q: You spoke of abstaining from other exercises when engaging in competition training. Is this really needed. I ride a jet-ski almost every day and love it. I can't imagine it hurting my training.

A: The body's healing reserves act just as a battery would. Multiply drains must not be placed on the battery when specific strengthening is being done. If you are having trouble understanding or believing the concept of the body's healing reserves acting as a battery, then I suggest the following test. Take two identical twins with the same diet and have them specifically train for arm strength with weights. Have one twin do nothing but the arm strengthening exercises and have the other add-in a seven mile daily jog. At the end of a year, take measurements of arm size size and strength. The differences will be staggering. The twin who added the long jogging session placed a secondary drain on the battery and payed the price. Just as you will with the jet-ski. Ask any surgeon how important it is to minimize activity after surgery to allow energy reserves to be solely focused on healing. This concept has not been lost on them.

Q: Do you have a favorite seat design?

A: My preference is for flat seat designs. Anything which has pronounced cupping creates a central ridge. I do not care for ridges.

Q: Very little in the way of numerical examples was given for the high-low training, or even fan vs test day training and how to advance, or where to start.

A: Yes, the given training regimens can be accurately described as open-ended and were designed to be so. These numbers are to be figured out through experimentation and proper estimates. The template is given and the math remains the responsibility of the competitor.

Q: Is there any other advice which can be given for competition day.

A: Yes, don't make the entire experience about competition. Talk to some people, make some friends, exchange emails and stay in touch with your fellow rowers. When you get into the city where the competition will be held, put on a rowing shirt to make yourself clearly visible. Rowers from all around the world will be converging around the competition area and nearby hotels. Rowers are generally in shape and look fantastic, but typically lack the extreme physical markers of sumo wrestlers, runway models and bodybuilders. Without these identifying flags, figuring out who is a rower and who is not, becomes utterly impossible; put on a rowing shirt. Remember, even if you are not competing, these events can still be attended. And for those competing, be sure to take someone along with you. You don't need a coach per se, but it's never really fun "going it" alone.

Q: Is the Tabata sprinting routine good for losing weight. I have heard of people advocating these sprints for weight reduction. How do they compare to the HIIT.

A: Questions regarding the fat burning potential of Tabata sprints keep coming up. Unfortunately, certain individuals fail to discern between Tabata and HIIT and oftentimes speak of "Tabata" fat burning effects, while foolishly citing HIIT-based research. The Tabata study did not measure fat burning. Regardless of unavailable data, it would be reasonable to assume that Tataba routines do in fact produce fat loss. But why would people favor them over the well studied HIIT routines? Half of the problem is ignorance; some people just don't know what HIIT is! The other problem deals with the strength of youth and the lazy factor. With youth comes stronger muscles and what oftentimes results is a preference for the "Tabata" routine. Why, well..... the principle reason is one of shortness. While more intense in the short run, Tabata routines are far less grinding than HIIT. The HIIT routine's sprinting is less intense, but added together, proves itself to be more painful than Tabata. More total work is demanded with HIIT and this "grinding nature" generates a certain fear among the young and lazy. This behavioral pattern is one of the "modern-ized" young and strong. Go back a 100 years in time and a reversal of trends would be seen due to years of long, grinding manual labor work. Contemporary tendencies aside, the better question to ask is what creates better fat loss, Tabata or HITT. For those who have read the material up to this point, advocacy for shorter workouts, at highter intensities, has been very strong, but is there a point at which further shortening of workout times (Tabata style) brings forth decreasing results? I believe the answer is yes, -with superiority remaining with HIIT. But, why is superiority assumed with HIIT?

The answer lies with the "optimization peak," and more import-antly, HIIT being that peak! The perfect area at which muscle preser-vation, along the maximally decreased fat levels are to be had. In oth-er words, the best of both worlds. Assumptions in this case, are based on visual evidence of body "builds" of various competitive runners at differing distances. Mid-range track runners are the most ripped/vascular athletes and still manage to carry a good amount of muscle. Move downward in the distance (very short distance sprinters) and larger, smoother muscles are seen, but in general, less vascularity and definition. Move upward (1000+ meters(track)) and competitors become overly thin and gangly. In the end, if you were to compare the bodies of track runners to the body shape generated by the HIIT routine, the most similar would be competitors in the middle distance track events. These comparisons are somewhat weak due to an apples and oranges problem; comparing non-stop running (track) and a succession of sprints (HIIT) on a rowing machine, is highly questionable. Still yet, this comparison works in a roundabout way. Obviously, frequent use of Tabata intervals will result in the appearance of smooth and rounded musculature, but without the striking vascularity or what may be referred to as great cuts. Don't get me wrong, they will look good, -to the point of being amazing and this will especially be true when comparisons are made between them and average, everyday suburbanites. However, when comparing the builds of Tabata practitioners to those utilizing HIIT, stark differences will be seen in the HIIT group. The HIIT routine results in an appearance of being ripped to the bone while still maintaining a good amount muscle mass. Here we have the hidden treasure that everybody has been searching for!

Unlike the mid-range track runners, rowers using the HIIT routine will obtain far better body development. Is there a better comparison available? You bet there is! For men, the best example is that of an Olympic gymnast and for women, the best comparison is that of collegiate gymnasts. To gain a similar look, weightlifting will have to be added to the mix. For those wondering if such statements are legit, -they are and this is a perfect description of what the HIIT routine, with a little extra weightlifting can accomplish. Being built like a gymnast is not exactly bad, now is it? This is perfection as far as I'm concerned and when the smoke clears, I believe my assumptions surrounding the superiority of the HIIT will be proven correct. I truly believe HIIT to be the Holy Grail of the exercise world. It's what we have all been searching for. It's here, it's yours, ...now use it!

Q: Why did you write the first chapter and go into the whole crew team debacle?

A: There is a pervasive assumption of indoor rowing being inadequate, or inferior when compared to its aquatic parent. Rowing on the water is not all its cracked-up to be. In all honesty, I firmly believe indoor rowing to be far superior to rowing on the water. This, I believe a thousand times over.

Q: I have 75 pounds to lose and was wondering as to what would be the best regimen to undertake. I was thinking about starting with HIIT.

A: HIIT pulls fat from the body very quickly. With so much weight to lose, it would be better to do it slowly. Use the regular 20 minutes program (light rowing at first) to get most of the weight off and when coming within 20-30 pounds, give HIIT a try. Also keep in mind, sprints may actually be a little dangerous at elevated weight levels.

Q: You advocate lifting weights in conjunction with rowing, but doesn't this mean I will have to get a gym membership.

A: For those "opting out" of competition, weightlifting is advocated. And no, gym memberships are not necessary. Purchase the weights. If money is a problem, then buy them used. Garage sales and flee markets have weights galore and it's all dirt cheap. If money is still yet a problem, start doing body weight exercise. Push-ups, pull-ups and squats are all good. If finding yourself under challenged, start switching to one arm push-ups, one arm pull-ups and the like.

As mentioned before, I detest the gym atmosphere. When inside a gym, you are breathing air at a quickened rate. This sets up a situation whereby pathogens can be spread and acquired at highly increased speeds. Adding to the problem, hordes people are coming in-and-out all day long and this alone increases exposure risk. What you can catch ranges from the flu to fungal infections and a whole lot of things in-between. Unfortunately, the "in-between" part now consists of highly drug-resistant and very dangerous strains of tuberculosis and staph. And what will be next to emerge is anyone's guess. People inside gyms are sweating, their pores are opened up and bronchial passages are functioning at full capacity. Small cuts and abrasions, which are very common for athletes, now make way for the aforementioned infections. Essentially, your body is placed in a very vulnerable and transmissive state. Your fully "opened-up" and touching every piece of sweat soaked equipment and breathing in the air from from every person in the place. It would be difficult to design a more perfect atmosphere or set of conditions for spreading viruses, bacteria, or fungi. When looking at gyms, the only thing I see are giant Petri dishes. An alarmist mentality is never beneficial, but certain admittances regarding newly emerging bugs can no longer be sidestepped.

Q: Is there any disabled group that can really benefit from rowing?

A: Yes, the blind. The blind oftentimes have to engage in exercises at a reduced intensity level, or have to engage in exercises specifically designed for their condition. This amounts to a situation whereby they are not experiencing various activities in the same manner as non-handicapped individuals. With rowing, the body is locked-in and it is almost all feel. Many people actually row with their eyes closed. As would be expected, specially adapted monitors have been designed for the blind. Blind rowers can compete and train with other non-blind rowers with no problem whatsoever. There is no difference between blind vs. non-blind rowers. Very few exercises can claim this!

Q: I have heard of paraplegics rowing. Could you please explain this?

A: Yes, this is true and I would be happy to give a brief overview. Using modified Concept2 machines, by way of high-back chairs, straps and additional leg stabilizers, -paraplegics can now row with the rest us. Upon first observation, certain happenings are almost imperceptible and casual glances prove to be deceptive. Some (not all) of these paraplegics are actually utilizing their legs! Yes, I mean actually utilizing, - "as in" fully contracting their leg muscles! How is this even remotely possible? Stick a few electrodes over the skin, zap the nerves and ta-dah, the dehumanizing effects of a spinal cord injury have now been nullified. The technology of Functional Electrical Stimulation or "FES" for short, is very well known and very old (discovered at the dawn of the modern medical era), but only in the last couple of years has it been "properly" coupled with rowing. Figuring out the angles, requirements for stabilization, electronics and underlining programming took a good bit of experimentation. Scientists are still fine tuning certain factors with regard to timing and firing sequences, but the technology is here and functioning. I will not go into any long diatribes regarding the importance (on so many levels) of this advancement; the situation speaks for itself. If you are interested in reading more on this subject, Concept2 has a nice article which can serve as a starting point: http://tinyurl.com/3xgtph. Additionally, a newsgroup for adaptive rowing can be signed up for by emailing to the following address:

AdaptiveRowingsubscribe@yahoogroups.com

References

1. Trembblay A, Simoneau JA, Bouchard C. Impact of Exercise Intensity on Body Fatness and Skeletal Muscle Metablism, Metabolism. 43(7): 814-818, (1994).

2. Tabata, Izumi, et al., "Metabolic profile of high intensity intermittent exercises," Medicine & Science in Sports & Exercise. 29(3):390-395, (1997).

3. G.B. Forbes, et al., "Hormonal Response to Overfeeding," American Journal of Clinical Nutrition. 49.4 : 608-611, (1989).

45418788R00117

Made in the USA
Middletown, DE
03 July 2017